teaching secondary
HOW SCIENCE WORKS ◆

Vanessa Kind
Per Morten Kind

HODDER
EDUCATION
PART OF HACHETTE UK

The Publishers would like to thank the following for permission to reproduce copyright material:

Acknowledgements Age standardised annual mortality rate and infant mortality rate graphs, Griffiths, C. and Brock A, (2003) 'Twentieth century mortality trends in England and Wales' *Health Statistics Quarterly* 18:5-17; Eskimo culture description of Earth and Northern Lights, Hawkes, E.W. (1926) *The Labrador Eskimo*. Ottaw: Geological Survey; Numbers of people dying of infectious diseases in England and Wales 1925-65 Marks, J. M. (1983) *Science and the Making of the Modern World* p.306); The case of the martian stone - 'NASA to revise space missions to focus on Mars findings (August 7, 1996) From the CNN website http://www.cnn.com/TECH/9608/07/mars.9p/ ; What causes the northern lights?- Visible spectrum of the aurora. and sunspots graphs, Egeland, A., Henriksen, E. and Henriksen T. (1997). Nordlys. Temahefte 3. Oslo: Department of Physics, University of Oslo; The mortality of doctors in relation to their smoking habits, Richard Doll and A. Bradford Hill (1954) British Medical Journal 1(4877): 1451 – 1455; Richard Doll interview text, British Lung Foundation, Origin Publishing,

Although every effort has been made to ensure that website addresses are correct at time of going to press, Hodder Education cannot be held responsible for the content of any website mentioned in this book. It is sometimes possible to find a relocated web page by typing in the address of the home page for a website in the URL window of your browser.

Hachette UK's policy is to use papers that are natural, renewable and recyclable products and made from wood grown in sustainable forests. The logging and manufacturing processes are expected to conform to the environmental regulations of the country of origin.

Orders: please contact Bookpoint Ltd, 130 Milton Park, Abingdon, Oxon OX14 4SB. Telephone: (44) 01235 827720. Fax: (44) 01235 400454. Lines are open 9.00–5.00, Monday to Saturday, with a 24-hour message answering service. Visit our website at www.hoddereducation.co.uk

©Vanessa Kind, Per Morten Kind 2008
First published in 2008 by
Hodder Education,
Hachette Company UK
338 Euston Road
London NW1 3BH

Impression number   5 4 3
Year   2013   2012

Cover photo: DNA anaylsis, TEK Image/Science Photo Library
Typeset in 12pt Galliard by Pantek Arts Ltd, Maidstone, Kent.
Printed by CPI Group (UK) Ltd, Croydon, CR0 4YY

A catalogue record for this title is available from the British Library

ISBN: 978 0340 941393

Contents

Acknowledgements

We are very grateful to Katie Mackenzie-Stuart, publisher, who has been patient and supportive throughout the writing process. We also thank David Sang, the series editor, for his wise comments about draft chapters that helped shape our ideas more concisely. We are extremely grateful to Helen Adamson, science teacher at Haydon Bridge School in Northumberland, for providing detailed comments and very helpful feedback on our draft chapters. Her significant scientific expertise and experiences on the Durham PGCE course helped to ensure that the book considers a newly qualified science teacher's perspective.

Vanessa Kind
Per Morten Kind
Durham
September 2007

Introduction

This book adds to the series of ASE handbooks. It was written to support teachers in delivering the latest version of the Science National Curriculum, which includes Programme of Study statements relating to how science works (DfES, 2004). In this introductory chapter we set out what a reader will find in the book and how to make best use of the material.

At the outset, we point out that this handbook is both similar to and different from earlier books in the series. Like the others, it contains activities for teachers to use in lessons. However, as this topic is less well defined and documented than others, we also include background information to provide readers with material from which their own understanding could be developed. We felt that simply providing an activities book was insufficient, as our experience suggests that more in-depth explanations will provide more secure support and enhance the benefit of the book for readers.

An introduction to how science works

The Science National Curriculum currently features four 'how science works' elements in the Programme of Study:

- data, evidence, theories and explanations
- practical and enquiry skills
- communication skills
- applications and implications of science.

Practical and enquiry skills are addressed thoroughly through published schemes, so we have, for the most part, not addressed those here. Our focus is on helping teachers to understand and teach the remaining three aspects.

We acknowledge that all science teachers have a subject matter background, normally centred in one of the three main areas of science. To teach how science works, we think that basic understanding of the meta-sciences – philosophy, history, psychology or sociology of science – is needed. We don't claim great expertise, but offer our own knowledge, slant and interpretations in the hope that others may benefit.

This is not just intended as another book on the philosophy of science. It is intended as a handbook with ideas, and advice on how ideas may be presented in the classroom to students. We hope that teachers can browse through it and find something constructive for that elusive last lesson of the day.

Outline of the book

The book opens with philosophies of science. This chapter has two purposes – to introduce teachers to their own implicit, embedded ideas about how science works, and to consider how these influence their practice. The first activity is for teachers. We strongly recommend that the background information in this chapter is read at some stage, as it sets the context for the rest of the book. If it appears indigestible in one sitting, try reading a small section every now and then.

Overall, the first chapter sets out science as a 'black box' activity. The black box is known to contain something, the nature of which is unknown. The task of science is to find out what is in the box and how it works.

Following philosophies are six chapters on how science works topics. These are selected for their relevance to the National Curriculum. Each stands alone, although cross-references are made to other chapters.

Scientific developments

Here we look at how scientific knowledge progresses. This includes considering science over a long, historical perspective, taking into account the change from informal, social knowledge to scientific theories. We try to convey the nature of scientific discovery – why and how this happens, using an example from each of pure and applied science. Underlying this is the perspective that science is not a fully told story. We challenge students to think about future science developments and questions that science cannot answer.

Scientific theories

In science, students are used to thinking *with* science theories, but not *about* them – they regard theories as descriptions rather than ideas. Science lessons tend to describe scientific theories rather than to explain them or discuss what they are like. In this chapter, we unpick the variety of meanings of the term scientific theory, and set these in the context of research on children's ideas.

Scientific evidence

The requirement for science to be based on evidence gained through experiment (or to be empirical in nature) is unique to this human endeavour. Evidence is collected through experiments following particular rules and procedures, commonly called the scientific method. We give examples of how this works, but also indicate that science is not entirely a rule-bound activity. We review research on children's understanding about experiments to provide supporting background material.

Scientific creativity

We show scientific creativity as an essential trait that is part of how science works, examining genius, logic, chance and *zeitgeist* (the spirit of the age) as contributing factors. We find this approach gives a realistic dimension to how science works, illustrating the roles genius scientists play, and how crucial discoveries can rely on logic. We try to redress the balance about chance discoveries, highlighting that these can't be made by anyone, but require scientists whose knowledge and skills are able to take advantage of chance events.

Ethics

The way in which scientific discoveries stimulate ethical dilemmas for society is well documented. We offer our suggestions for approaching this aspect of handling scientific ethics. In addition, we examine ethical practice in science. We describe how scientists attempt to police themselves, setting out ethics for practice. We also give examples of scientists whose behaviour stepped outside these unwritten rules. The reminder here is that the practice of science is a human activity that relies not just on theories, evidence and explanations.

Error, risk and hazard

Science generates more dilemmas than just ethical ones – hazards and risks are apparent in scientific activities, just as they are in any other profession. Here we show occasions when scientists were not sufficiently aware of the hazards and risks associated with their work, resulting occasionally in devastating situations. Helping students assess risk accurately and wisely is considered – we offer activities and discussion that may help achieve this.

Structure of the chapters

◆ *Activities*

In setting out the activities, for the most part we have followed the now traditional three-part format so that teachers can find a complete lesson's worth of material by reading a few pages. We didn't want to be slaves to this format, though, as it can become stilted and prohibit teachers' own inventiveness and creativity. So in places we have written activities that can be slotted into a scheme of work.

The activities have been designed specifically to pick up issues relating to how science works. This may sound obvious, but bears some explanation, as the questions and style of the tasks may seem unusual at times. The reason for this is that we have tried to get at what is going on underneath, in science process terms, rather than focusing on surface descriptions of phenomena. The extent of our success can only be determined by the reader and user.

Throughout the book we have tried to take a novel approach by viewing familiar material from new angles, as in activities on the thalidomide tragedy (Chapter 7) and the link between smoking and lung cancer (Chapter 5). Writing about how science works has also given us the freedom to introduce some entirely new material that, as far as we are aware, is not commonly taught, such as that on modern-day scientific geniuses (Chapter 5), understanding the northern lights (Chapter 2), and how the Earth's surface features form (Chapter 3). At times we stretch the limits of knowledge required for Key Stage 4, but we believe this is justified as students often want to know more, and the curriculum is a minimum entitlement – there is nothing to say that teachers can't step outside this.

For ease of use, the Programme of Study statements that the activity is designed to meet are identified. These are summarised in the table on page *xiii*. Almost all activities have associated worksheets as pdfs on the accompanying CD ROM. In the places where we have stretched academic limits, we have provided easier alternatives. Elsewhere we leave judging the level of difficulty to teachers.

Tables and boxes provided throughout the book are also intended for teachers to use in lessons. These will provide contextual detail that can enrich an activity. Some boxes offer 'story' material – the ability to tell a good story can be useful to capture attention and to introduce, embellish or conclude a lesson.

A final point about the activities is that we do not intend them to be set in stone, but to provide stimulation for teachers who find their own ideas more valuable for their students. The tasks can be read as suggestions. For example, the same general points about ethics in Chapter 6 could be asked of other contexts than the four dilemmas we present. Other theories than explanations for the northern lights can be put in a timeline to illustrate jumps in development (Chapter 2). Of course, one reason for having pre-prepared activities is to reduce preparation time, but we hope that readers will feel inspired to research for themselves areas of science that they or their students find particularly appealing.

◆ *Background information*

We have written the background information with the aim of providing support for teachers who wish to develop their own knowledge in this area. It is not essential to read this as the activities stand alone, but we hope that teachers will want to know more. We have included different types of background material depending on the topic. For example, the chapters on theories (Chapter 3) and evidence (Chapter 4) review research on children's ideas about these topics. Chapter 2, on philosophies of science, is intended primarily for teachers to learn about these and to consider their own science teaching approach. Chapter 5, on creativity, will almost certainly challenge the thinking of teachers whose approach has been to think 'arts and science' when they hear this word. Elsewhere, we provide information that may seem basic to some readers, but novel to others. Overall, we have tried to generate a mini-compendium of material that we would appreciate using for our own teaching.

◆ *References and resources*

Past experience of preparing materials for teachers suggests that resource lists are often widely used. We have been as thorough as possible in providing websites that are current and useful. All websites in the text were functioning at the time of writing. Academic references that can be difficult to obtain have been kept to a minimum.

We have not referenced every single piece of information in the book – in many cases we would not know where to find this, because we have recalled material that we have learned over long periods. We are also aware of condensing large areas of science into short texts, and the omissions this entails. Direct quotes and specific source materials are referenced. We have made every effort to check these details. We apologise for any remaining errors and omissions and would be pleased to correct these if they are drawn to the attention of the publisher.

How best to use the book

We have written the book for use in different ways. We want teachers to read it and develop their own understanding about how science works, but it is also intended as:

♦ a resource book of activities
♦ a resource book of stories to supplement teaching of conceptual topics
♦ a book to illustrate teaching strategies appropriate for teaching how science works.

We also want teachers to transfer their own understanding about how science works into their teaching and into students' learning. Although we supply specific teaching strategies and activities, we do not think there is one recipe for how to teach about science successfully. If, as a result of reading all or part of this book, teachers reflect on what it means to teach about science, we will have achieved our aim.

References

DfES (2004) *Science in the National Curriculum*. London: The Stationery Office

Programme of Study statements

Section	Activity	Page no.	1a	1b	1c	1d	2a	2b	2c	2d	3a	3b	3c	4a	4b	4c
1.2	The Card Exchange						Activity for teachers									
1.2	Tricky tracks						X			X						
1.2	Black box activities		X	X	X											
2.2	What causes the northern lights?			X	X					X						
2.2	Declining death, improving health										X	X	X			
2.2	How does the stomach work?		X	X	X		X	X								
2.2	What do scientists know? What remains to be found out?					X									X	X
3.2	The development of atomic theory		X	X												X
3.2	How true is a theory?				X											
3.2	Theories and evidence				X											
4.2	A hypothesis that was proved wrong – how the Earth's features were formed				X						X		X			X
4.2	A hypothesis that was proved correct – the true cause of stomach ulcers				X									X		
4.2	A hypothesis that is inconclusive – the case of the Martian stone			X		X				X	X		X			
5.2	Using your creativity			X	X		X									
5.2	Chemical egg races						X	X	X							
5.2	The link between smoking and lung cancer			X							X					
5.2	What makes a genius scientist?												X			
6.2	General information about argumentation tasks													X	X	X
6.2	Whole-class debate														X	X
6.2	Small group discussions													X	X	X
6.3	The development of nuclear weapons													X	X	X
6.3	Using animals in experiments – their lives or ours?													X	X	X
6.3	Using human embryos – research at the edge of humanity														X	X
6.3	The development of genetically modified organisms – the latest style of lunch													X	X	X
7.2	Personal choice, personal risk		X											X		
7.2	Bad science, good science												X	X	X	X
7.2	MMR: what's the risk?									X				X		X
7.2	Bird flu in Burnham!											X		X	X	

How science works

1.1 Why do you need this chapter?

This is the chapter you may think about skipping, as its purpose may not seem obvious. If this is you, please reconsider. It aims to:

♦ encourage you to think about your own views about how science works, based on your background – this may or may not be based in science
♦ encourage your students to think about how science works – where scientific knowledge comes from
♦ show that scientific knowledge is constructed in a variety of ways, not just through 'scientific method'

The first activity helps to meet the first aim. It gives you the opportunity to reflect on how the varied backgrounds of science teachers may influence teaching. The activity can also be done with older students, but its purpose is to help clarify and challenge teachers' ideas about how science works. The activity shows that science is varied and there is no one 'correct vision' of a 'scientist'.

Activities with students are provided to help meet the second aim. These encourage thinking of science as a 'black box' – something is known to be inside, but to find out what, scientists must experiment. This sets the scene for how science is done – and tries to encourage teachers to think in an **investigative** rather than a **descriptive** way when teaching. Science thus comprises problems requiring solutions rather than being based on learning facts and describing objects. Scientists may disagree – alternative methods and solutions are possible.

The third aim involves reading about science as seen through five philosophers. We illustrate that science began, in the Anglophone countries, with belief in one "scientific method" (Bacon and Popper). Agreeing on a scientific method, was important for the political purpose of establishing science as a subject above superstition. Aspects of this are still seen in school science today – traditionally, science is taught as a practical subject, involving constructing hypotheses, doing experiments and drawing conclusions (see Popper and Chapter 5). However, we show through three more philosophers, Kuhn, Lakatos and

Feyerabend, that many people believe 'scientific method' provides a basic training only in how to collect evidence; and that science knowledge is based on more than data and experiment. The philosophers differ from each other, but all suggest that social processes such as argument, debate, discussion and resolution of controversies contribute to constructing new scientific knowledge. Understanding this variety is essential for understanding how science works.

1.2 Activities

♦ *The Card Exchange: establishing your own views about the nature of science (teacher activity)*

This activity provides an opportunity for science teaching colleagues to consider their views about how science works, and to debate these with others. The activity was originally designed for groups of 20 or more – we have presented the original version, but as most science departments are smaller, we also suggest modifications. The activity may also be a good ice-breaker for post-16 students beginning an AS science course. The activity is taken from Cobern and Loving (1998).

Original version – for groups of about 20

Purpose
To establish what science is all about – and to test your views about this against those of others.

Preparation
- ♦ Make a set of cards using the statements provided on the CD. Make sure that a broad range of viewpoints is represented – feel free to add statements to suit, but for a large group it is a good idea to keep the variety.
- ♦ Ensure that there are enough cards so that colleagues are not stuck with statements they cannot agree with – allow for some cards to be redundant.
- ♦ For a group of 20, the original authors suggest preparing 200 cards – 40 different cards, five copies of each.
- ♦ Shuffle the cards thoroughly.

To play the game

1. The leader deals up to eight cards at random to each player (for 20 people, eight cards each will leave 40 cards unused).
2. Players read the statements on their cards and decide how far they agree with them.
3. Players mingle with each other and start to exchange cards, swapping statements they don't like or don't agree with for those they prefer. Cards cannot be discarded. Allow about 10 minutes for this.
4. Return players to their seats. They should now have a set of statement cards with which they broadly agree.
5. Next, instruct the players to mingle again, but this time they must form a pair. The pair must hold between them eight cards on which both members agree. Each member must contribute at least three cards. Through discussion, players must reach a compromise as to which cards must be kept. The remaining cards can be discarded.
6. Now each pair must find another pair, making a quartet. Again, the quartet must hold eight cards, at least three coming from each pair. The remaining cards are discarded. The quartet must then rank the eight cards and can disregard the two lowest-ranked cards.
7. Each quartet must write a paragraph summarising their view about the nature of science, as agreed and shown by the card statements.
8. The paragraphs are shared with the whole group, each quartet indicating why they accepted and rejected certain statements.

The task is likely to generate some discussion, so be prepared for a forthright exchange of opinion.

The statements

Forty statements are provided on the CD, divided into categories:

♦ theoretical emphasis – science is rational and theory-driven (1–6)
♦ empirical emphasis – science involves data-gathering and experimental work to collect physical evidence (7–13)
♦ anti-science view – science is over-rated; we should not give too much credence to what scientists say, or to the methods, results or aims of science (14–20)
♦ scientism – science is the perfect discipline, the highest form of knowing (21–27)

♦ cultural view – science is embedded in our cultures, which provide a social, historical and psychological background to scientists' work (28–34)
♦ balanced view – science is a complicated affair, there is no single scientific method, science cannot be reduced to a few simple descriptive statements (35–40).

Adapting the Card Exchange for smaller numbers

Here are several ways in which the Card Exchange can be adapted for smaller numbers.

1. Scale down the number of cards prepared. Use the same set of 40 statements, but prepare fewer copies of each. For a group of 10, for example, prepare 120 cards – 40 cards, three copies of each.
2. Stop the game at the pair stage. Each pair has to write a paragraph summarising their views of science.
3. Cut the number of statements to 20 or 30. Produce one set of cards for each group of four participants. Each group has to select nine cards that best summarise their views about science, then arrange these into a 'diamond nine' formation: 1, 2, 3, 2, 1 cards in rows, from their most important statement at the top to their least important at the bottom.
4. Select around 20 statements, a few from each category, and present these in a list format. Colleagues either work singly or discuss in pairs the extent to which they agree or disagree with the statements, coming up with a paragraph that summarises their view of the nature of science. These are then discussed.

Closing discussion

Discuss any different views about science expressed in the concluding paragraphs. Questions to consider include the following.

♦ Do views fall along subject lines? Do biology-based colleagues hold different views from physics specialists? Where do the chemists fit in?
♦ Do colleagues with industry-based/other backgrounds have different views?
♦ What were the most difficult and easiest statements to discard?
♦ What compromises had to be made?
♦ How might teachers' views on how science works affect students' learning about science?

◆ *Introducing students to how science works*

We suggest activities that introduce key aspects of science: the difference between observation and inference, the tentativeness of scientific knowledge and the role of creativity in science. These are based on those suggested by Lederman and Abd-El-Khalick (1998).

◆ *Tricky tracks – making observations and inferences*

Time required: about 30 minutes total
NC link: 2a, d

Learning outcomes

- ◆ To understand the difference between observation and inference.
- ◆ To understand what 'making an observation' means.
- ◆ To realise that observations can be prejudiced.

Starter activity

Many students are likely to watch crime shows, of which CSI (Crime Scene Investigation) is probably the most topical at the time of writing. Invite discussion as to how the crimes are solved – what evidence is collected and what conclusions (inferences) are drawn? How certain are the investigators that they have solved the crime correctly? What happens if they get it wrong?

The CSI website (www.cbs.com/primetime/csi) gives plotlines and a handbook with details of the kinds of evidence collected.

Main activity

Time required: about 20 minutes' whole-class discussion

The points below lead you through a discussion using Figures A–C (provided on the CD). The order in which they are presented and the questions you ask are important to the success of the activity. You can also present the figures in sequence (see CD).

1. Show Figure C (see CD). Ask students to write down what they think might have happened, based on what they see. This is important, as students will be able to judge the validity of their statements more easily if they have written them down. They should set this aside until the end.

2. Now show Figure A (see CD). Ask 'What do you observe?' Accept all answers without judgement. List answers for future reference. 'Bird (or other animal) tracks', 'tracks left by birds', 'birds walking to the same spot' are expected responses.

3. Next, ask, 'Can you see the birds?' and 'How do you know these are bird tracks?' Clarify that 'they are produced by birds' is an **inference** – the tracks could be made by dinosaurs, or simply be marks on the screen.

4. Ask, 'Why were the two animals going to the same spot?' Answers may include – finding water, going for the same prey, one attacking the other, going to a high point to take off, etc. Again, all these are inferences. There is no evidence for any of them. All are possible scenarios.

5. Now show Figure B (see CD). Ask again, 'What do you observe?' This time the tracks are mingled. Some may say 'the birds are fighting' (inference); 'the birds are mating' (inference); 'the birds are going for the same prey' (inference). Each inference is valid from the evidence. Make the point that 'the tracks are mingled' is an observation.

6. Show Figure C again, and ask again, 'What do you observe?' This time hope for the response 'The marks are mingled and only the larger set is left' – an observation. Then ask 'What do you infer?' Again, a range of responses is possible, including: 'the larger bird ate the smaller one', 'the larger bird is carrying the smaller one', or 'the small bird flew away'. Once again, each inference is valid from the evidence.

7. Now return students to their written statements. What do they think now, after the class discussion? Did they write observations or inferences? Can we ever really know, based on evidence, what happened?

Plenary discussion

Finally, make explicit two points:

♦ the difference between observation and inference
♦ many different inferences are possible from one piece of evidence.

The overall point is that scientists work from observations and make inferences from them. Observations can be prejudiced by what we have in our mind beforehand. Also, scientists may never know in some cases whether their inferences are right or wrong.

Other points to consider

♦ The figures could also be used in order A–C – asking students to make observations and draw conclusions about each one as it is shown. The responses will need to be modified each time a new figure is seen, showing that scientists have to modify their beliefs as more evidence is collected.

♦ Ensure that inferences are consistent with the evidence – students may suggest inferences that can't really be drawn from the figures. This emphasises the point that scientific knowledge is based on what we can observe by experiment, or empirical evidence.

♦ With older students, introduce the concept of time frame. There is no evidence that both tracks on any figure were produced at the same time – two creatures could have gone to the same spot independently of each other.

♦ There is no evidence that these are animal tracks at all. They could be just marks on a paper, drawn by someone. This line of discussion can be taken all the way to the idea that some concepts exist only in scientists' heads. There are links here to other parts of this book, for example, the 'life on Mars' activity (page 81) and the fraudulent behaviour of scientists (page 125) who wish their theories were true.

♦ *Black box activities – observation, inference and creativity*

Time required: 1 hour minimum – extendable
NC link: 1a, b, c

Learning outcomes

♦ To understand the difference between observation and inference.
♦ To realise that scientific knowledge is, at least partly, produced by humans using their imagination and creativity.
♦ To realise that scientific knowledge is generated by experiment and observation.
♦ To understand that scientific knowledge is subject to change.

Background

A black box activity imitates what scientists do. The activity gives students the chance to make observations, collect data, set up a hypothesis, test it and review it.

Starter

A suitable starter activity would be to identify objects hidden in 'feely bags'. These are bags made of soft fabric that can be opened at the neck. An object is placed inside. Students have to put one hand inside the bag to identify the object without seeing it. There are variations on this – a feely box, which is perhaps easier to prepare; or asking students to put on a blindfold and a pair of gloves then asking them to identify an object placed in their hands. These could be everyday items such as non-sharp kitchen or other home implements, or simple pieces of science equipment.

The point is to indicate that scientists work in the dark – when they start to investigate something, they do not know what it is they are looking at, but have to use evidence to work it out. Many phenomena cannot be seen – gravity, black holes, electricity, atoms, temperature, etc. Scientists are investigating 'black boxes'.

Main activity

Figures 1.1–1.3 illustrate three alternative black box activities from Lederman and Abd-El-Khalide (1998). Each shows a phenomenon – but does not reveal how it is produced. Students have to work out what is happening, and why.

Recycling water

Figure 1.1
Recycling water

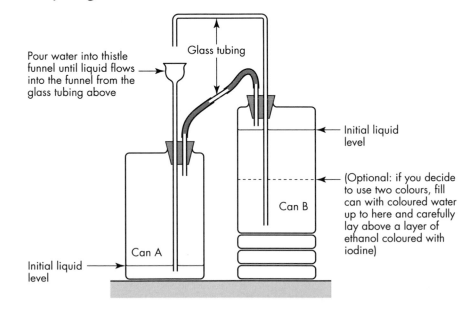

Requirements: two $500\,\text{cm}^3$ empty cans or conical flasks wrapped in foil; two stoppers; rubber tubing; one thistle funnel; glass tubing; ethanol, iodine, food colouring (optional).

Setting up: the levels of water and relative heights of the containers are adjusted so that pouring a relatively small amount of water in the lower can generates a self-perpetuating siphon, rather like a water feature in a garden. To add an unexpected feature, the higher container can be filled partly with coloured water, covered with a layer of ethanol coloured with iodine. This will generate a more complex pattern in the liquid flow.

The hypothesis box

Figure 1.2 *The hypothesis box*

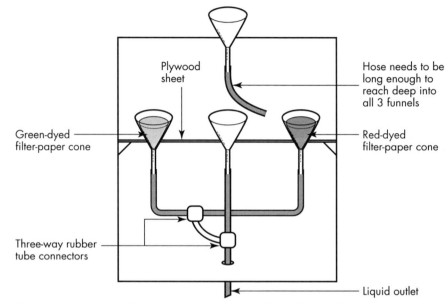

Plywood sheet

Hose needs to be long enough to reach deep into all 3 funnels

Green-dyed filter-paper cone

Red-dyed filter-paper cone

Three-way rubber tube connectors

Liquid outlet

Requirements: a box approximately $70 \times 50 \times 30$ cm, with an open back; one sheet of plywood or similar, about 50×30 cm; four funnels; rubber tubing; two three-way tubing connectors; two filter-paper cones; two different food colours/water-soluble dyes; several 250 cm^3 beakers; tap water.

Setting up: the aim is to allow students to see only the top funnel and the outlet tube. The arrangement of the three other funnels and tubing remains hidden. The teacher can vary the position of the free tube, pointing it into any one of the three other funnels. In preparation, take care that the tubing will stretch to all three funnels. When water is poured into the top funnel, the hypothesis box will produce different-coloured water from the outlet, depending on the funnel it passes through. The wooden sheet can be used to cover up the back of the box while the water is running through.

The water-making machine

Figure 1.3 *The water-making machine*

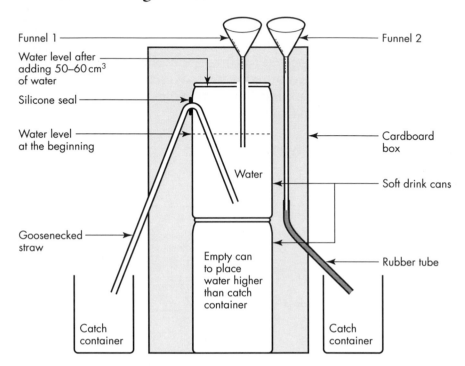

Funnel 1
Funnel 2
Water level after adding 50–60 cm³ of water
Silicone seal
Water level at the beginning
Cardboard box
Water
Soft drink cans
Goosenecked straw
Empty can to place water higher than catch container
Rubber tube
Catch container
Catch container

Requirements: a box, approximately $35 \times 25 \times 15$ cm (e.g. an adult shoe box); two empty 300 cm³ cans; one drinking straw with a bendy neck; two 500 cm³ beakers; two funnels; rubber tubing; sealant.

Setting up: ensure the bottom of the straw is close to the base of the can, and that the straw is sealed effectively at the side of the can. The machine is primed before the lesson by pouring 270 cm³ water into funnel 1. The class is told that the machine will 'make water' – if 60 cm³ is poured into funnel 1, then 330 cm³ will be produced. The second funnel acts as a dummy – if water is poured in here, then only the amount poured in will be recovered. This tells us that there is something special about the other funnel.

Running the activity

♦ Preparing and testing the activity thoroughly prior to the lesson is vital.
♦ Decide how much time you want to allow – to take this as far as possible, the activity may need to run over more than one lesson. This would allow students time to develop their own models and drawings.

Step 1: Introduce the phenomenon

Say that you have something that demonstrates a phenomenon. The class must act as scientists to work out what is happening.

Ask students to make observations and inferences. Check they understand the difference (see page 5–6). Make sure that their inferences are consistent with their observations.

For Recycling water –
Observation: 'Water is flowing from the tube above the funnel'
Inference: 'Water is moving between the two cans/flasks' – this cannot be seen

For The hypothesis box –
Observation: 'The water changes colour'
Inference: 'Something inside the box gives colour to the water'

For The water-making machine –
Observation: 'More water came out than went in'
Inference: 'There was water inside the machine already'

Step 2: Make hypotheses

- Ask students to suggest hypotheses to explain how the phenomenon works. Invite them to discuss their ideas with the class.
- Judge whether the hypotheses are consistent with the data.
- Accept all hypotheses that are consistent with the data, and reject others.

Step 3: Test hypotheses

- Ask students to think about how they could test their hypotheses. For example, with the water-making machine, if they think water was in the machine already, colouring the water that is poured in would generate a diluted colour in the receiver.
- Ask if they think hypotheses can truly be proven. Evidence only adds support to a hypothesis. Until we open the box, we can never know.
- The water-making machine discussion could be continued with the idea that as the machine only makes water, of course the dye would be diluted!

Step 4: Make models

To take this to its limits, ask students to make models explaining how the phenomenon might work. This shows how limited scientists are – they do the same in explaining phenomena. We can never really know what happens inside a black box – we use evidence from experiment to get a best-fit model.

We pick up this point in Chapter 3, which looks at theories (page 58).

Students' interest may have waned by this point, so there is no need to labour it – a quick sketch or outline from some would make the point.

Plenary discussion

♦ Draw out that the black box represents a phenomenon that scientists are trying to understand. They can't open the box – for example, we can't open an atom to find out what is inside. All scientists can do is collect evidence by experiment and draw conclusions from that.
♦ Draw out the way scientists work – they need to be imaginative, creative and careful in what they do. Knowledge is tentative and not reliable – it can change. Scientists need to keep an open mind that takes in new ideas.

1.3 Background information

In this section we review different philosophies of science.

♦ *Early philosophies*

How science works and how knowledge makes progress has provided philosophical thinkers with much material over time. Various ancient cultures proposed that all matter was made from a small set of elements. In Western culture, we are most familiar with the suggestion made by the ancient Greek philosopher Empedocles. He suggested that everything came from the 'roots' (later called elements) earth, air, fire and water. Aristotle added 'aether' or ether as a fifth element specifically to describe the material from which stars and heavenly bodies were made.

Elsewhere, other cultures proposed similar ideas, each with an individual twist. It is thought that Buddha proposed the four-element theory before the Greeks, teaching that these were the basis for understanding suffering. Buddha's teachings were probably taken by messengers to other cultures around the world, whose peoples adapted them slightly. The Chinese, who were Taoists, added wood as a fifth element, while the Japanese added 'void', meaning 'something not of our everyday life'. The native Maoris in New Zealand added 'flora' as their fifth element. However the word got around, or whether the same proposal was made at different places in the world at the same time, the four-element theory set the scene for scientific thinking for about 2000 years, persisting through Western Europe's Middle Ages. The philosopher Francis Bacon lived at a time when science had just begun to move away from reliance on this very basic theory.

◆ *Francis Bacon – induction and logical deduction*

Box 1.1 Francis Bacon, 1561–1626

Francis Bacon was born in London in 1561, the son of Nicolas Bacon, the Lord Keeper of the Seal (a post usually part of the role of Lord Chancellor) in Elizabeth I's reign. He studied law at Trinity College Cambridge, aged 12, continuing at Gray's Inn, one of London's four Inns of Court, aged 15. His father died in 1579, leaving him, as the second son of a second marriage, without financial support. Nevertheless, Bacon qualified as a lawyer, working initially as a lecturer in law. He became a Member of Parliament in 1584, with ambitions of greatness. Bacon offended Elizabeth I by opposing her new tax regime in 1593, effectively curtailing his career under her rule. When James I became King in 1603, Bacon's fortunes changed. He was knighted, then appointed to a series of high offices, including Attorney General in 1613, his father's old job, Lord Keeper of the Seal in 1617 and, in 1618, Lord Chancellor, a position of great power. Having achieved success, Bacon made a catastrophic error: in 1621 he was found to have accepted a bribe, so he ended up imprisoned in the Tower of London. He was eventually released, then returned to the family estate in Hertfordshire where he died in 1626.

Bacon's scientific career was really a hobby, science being just one of his many interests. He is also known as a historian, essayist and intellectual reformer, and has been proposed as the 'true' author of Shakespeare's plays.

Bacon's philosophy of science

Bacon based his ideas about the nature of science on induction and logical deduction. This involves making general statements based on observations. For example, if we investigate sodium chloride, a reasonable statement based on observations of its appearance is 'sodium chloride is crystalline'. We have deduced this logically by observation, having some idea what we mean by 'crystalline'. Studying a few more crystalline solids may lead us to claim more generally that 'all solids are crystalline'. This statement is not based on actually examining all possible solids, but on the few examples tested. Bacon uses the word 'induction' to describe how a statement is extended from applying to a few known examples to being true for all. Another statement, 'all white solids are crystalline', would, by logical deduction and without doing any further tests, also be true. This is because the general statement 'all solids are crystalline' also applies to any white solid. So we have three types of statement making a chain, called by Bacon the 'ladder of intellect':

♦ sodium chloride is crystalline – specific observation
♦ all white solids are crystalline – middle level
♦ all solids are crystalline – general level.

The general statement is contradicted by finding a non-crystalline solid. A white non-crystalline solid also contradicts the middle-level statement. Bacon was aware of this possibility, so he proposed that the most general statement should not be reached until middle-level ones, such as 'all white solids are crystalline', were thoroughly tested. To test 'all white solids are crystalline' thoroughly would, in theory, require investigation of every existing solid, as well as defining 'crystalline', 'solid' and 'white' satisfactorily. This would be impossible, as we could never be certain that all had been tested. Rather than testing them all, we have to use induction. Bacon argued that this process would create an unshakeable 'edifice of knowledge'. He said, as a Lord Chancellor might, 'knowledge is power'.

Bacon's views use observations to make deductions and then, by induction, establish facts:

observation → deduction → induction.

We make observations by doing experiments or observing nature. Bacon is described as an empiricist because he proposed that scientific knowledge comes directly from experience.

Bacon's ideas are apparent today: one of the authors was taught 'test, observation, inference' while doing ordinary-level chemistry in the 1970s, a sequence with a definite Baconian air. Today, making observations and drawing conclusions are emphasised when helping young students with their first experiences of science – perhaps another echo of Bacon reverberating down the centuries.

Faults with Bacon's philosophy

Bacon's philosophy has been rejected for many reasons, including the following.

♦ How can we make observations of phenomena we can't see? Gravity can't be seen; particles and microbes can only be seen with powerful microscopes. If we don't see or experience the phenomenon, only its effects, we can't observe objectively.

♦ Observations are not prejudice-free – we do not see objectively. For example, chemists differ about the colour of a precipitate such as copper(I) oxide. This compound, produced in a positive Fehling's test for a reducing sugar such as glucose, may be described as orange, red, reddy-orange, orangey-red, or ochre.

♦ What is worth observing is open to discussion – scientists may not agree what makes worthwhile events, phenomena or situations for gathering observations. There is no guarantee that an 'edifice of knowledge' truly represents nature.

♦ The principle of induction is flawed – at what point should an observer claim that what is being examined applies generally? After 50 experiments? 100? 1000? This problem of induction – turning observations based on a few examples into universal laws – was explored further by the eighteenth-century philosopher David Hume in his *Treatise on Human Nature*, written in 1739.

♦ There is no evidence that any great scientific discovery has ever been made using Bacon's ideas. Although many scientists have painstakingly recorded data, genuine scientific progress has involved another factor, such as creative insight. Collecting observations alone has not generated new knowledge, other than the observations themselves.

◆ *Karl Popper – the scientific method*

Box 1.2 Karl Popper, 1902–94

Karl Raimund Popper was born in Vienna, Austria, the son of a lawyer. Karl's upbringing was bookish: Popper's father was interested in classics, philosophy and social and political issues, while his mother had a passion for music. Popper qualified first as a primary school teacher (1925), then gained a PhD (1928) and finally trained to teach secondary maths and physics (1929). Popper heard Einstein lecture on his relativity theory, contrasting this favourably with the way writers such as Karl Marx discussed their work. Popper was on the fringes of the Viennese circle, a group of intellectuals discussing science and philosophy. He became increasingly critical of the group's stance, developing his own thinking that led to publication of the first version of *The Logic of Scientific Discovery* in 1934. In the 1930s Popper worked as a schoolteacher, escaping Nazism by emigrating to New Zealand in 1937, where he lectured in philosophy at the University of Canterbury. In 1946, Popper moved to the London School of Economics in England, becoming professor in 1949. He was knighted in 1965 and made a Companion of Honour in 1982. Although Popper retired in 1969, he remained intellectually active until his death in 1994.

Popper is thought generally to have been a difficult character, arguing with everyone and failing to resolve situations that created bad feeling for many years. For example, he refused to allow the academic post he once occupied to be named after him in case it was given to someone with whom he had argued. Although criticism was a feature of his theories, he found this difficult to accept about his own work. Anyone, even the most devoted disciple, who dared to make the smallest suggestion about Popper's work risked causing lifelong offence. Nevertheless, Popper is regarded as one of the world's greatest philosophers, generating ideas in areas of science, social and political theory that won him many awards.

Popper's philosophy of science

Popper wanted to generate a philosophy of science that recognised and accounted for the achievements of acknowledged scientific greats such as Galileo, Kepler, Newton, Einstein and Bohr. He tried to account for how scientific knowledge develops, a point absent from Bacon's ideas. Popper's ideas are described in *The Logic of Scientific Discovery*, first published in German in 1934, and reformulated and published in English in 1959.

To understand Popper's thinking, let us go back to the 'white solids' example. Popper turns Bacon's thinking on its head, allowing us to make the statement 'all white solids are crystalline' up-front, without any proof. The statement can be right or wrong. We can assume it is correct until contradictory evidence is found. Popper used the word 'falsified' to describe such a statement – finding a white solid that is not crystalline or a solid that is crystalline but not white would falsify the statement. This removes the need for induction – we don't have to test 50 or 100 or even 1000 solids to prove the statement. Instead, Popper's philosophy allows scientists to make a statement, then to test its truth. The statement is a working principle, a tentative or testable theory that permits science to make progress. If we have to reject it, then perhaps another theory will stand more rigorous testing and fit a wider range of white substances. Even the most rigorously tested theory is still technically falsifiable – knowledge is held to be true only until a piece of evidence is produced that clearly contradicts it. Popper called his philosophy 'critical rationalism'.

Popper's scientific method is a process of recognising a problem, setting up a theory or theories that could explain it, rigorously testing these, rejecting faulty theories and establishing which best fit the obtainable evidence. The process cycles on as theories that started off as tentative gain acceptance, as supporting evidence accumulates. Theories develop and become established as 'fact' because no evidence falsifies them. New problems arise for further investigation. Popper's views of how science works are like natural selection – survival of the fittest theories leads to their acceptance as scientific knowledge. The strength of Popper's proposals lies in accepting tentative theories that are raw, untested products of human thinking. Einstein's theory of relativity, for example, was proposed as a 'thought experiment' that could be subject to testing and critical review. Thus scientific knowledge can progress by combining human intellect and experimental effort to resolve a problem.

Faults with Popper's scientific method

Popper's notions have been criticised. For example, one scientific theory cannot be tested alone, as each theory is set within other theories. What happens if we get evidence contradicting one theory in the structure? How do we handle such evidence? Here is an example that illustrates this problem:

- Nineteenth-century astronomers accepted that there were only seven planets as 'fact'. However, they observed that Uranus did not move in a way that obeyed Newton's law of gravitation. Based on these observations, Newton's law could be false. Eventually, astronomers agreed the odd movement was caused by an undiscovered planet interfering with Uranus. The planet was identified in 1846 and named Neptune. Instead of Newton's theory being false, the accepted fact was wrong.
- If the planet had not been found, what would have been the outcome? Perhaps other theories would have been proposed: for example, that the observations were caused by another factor, such as an asteroid belt, or the telescope was faulty. The point is that arriving at the right answer did not depend on falsifying one pre-existing theory.
- To get to the actual 'truth', scientists did more than look at the evidence – they used judgement. Judgement falls outside Popper's theory that falsification alone determines the development of scientific knowledge.

In practice, as this example shows, scientists don't seem to work by falsifying each other's theories. Instead, they collect evidence and consider the whole picture surrounding it, before deciding what to change.

◆ *Thomas Kuhn – scientific revolutions*

Kuhn's philosophy of science

Kuhn's main contribution to science philosophy is *The Structure of Scientific Revolutions* (1962). Kuhn describes science as 'a series of peaceful interludes punctuated by intellectually violent revolutions'. In those revolutions, he said, 'one conceptual world view is replaced by another'. He introduced the term 'paradigm' (pronounced 'paradime'), perhaps best described as a web or matrix of interconnected theories and ideas providing a framework supporting scientists' experiments. The paradigm is accepted by the scientific community until a major event occurs that promotes a paradigm shift.

Box 1.3 Thomas Kuhn, 1922–96

Thomas Samuel Kuhn was born in Cinncinnati, Ohio, USA in 1922. His father was an industrial engineer. Like Popper, Kuhn worked as an academic. He began by studying physics, graduating in 1943, in the middle of the Second World War. Kuhn spent the rest of the war researching radar, at the time a new development that contributed significantly to the Allied cause. Post-war, Kuhn did a PhD at Harvard in solid-state physics, gaining this in 1949. While there, Harvard's president, James B. Conant, suggested Kuhn teach an undergraduate course in humanities as part of students' general education in science. This involved using historical case studies. The study of scientific history was just developing as an academic discipline: Kuhn was captured. Kuhn realised on reading Aristotle's

work that he was not 'wrong' – from the Greek's own perspective, Aristotle's understanding of motion and matter were simply different from those of Newton. This provided Kuhn with the impetus to create a career in history and philosophy of science, subsequently taking up posts at America's best universities. In 1956 Kuhn moved west to the University of California at Berkeley, becoming professor in 1961, and then moved to New Jersey (in the east), to Princeton, in 1964. After 13 years there, he went to Massachusetts Institute of Technology in Boston, where he remained until his death from cancer in 1996.

Traditionally, science is thought to progress by adding new theories to knowledge, without dismissing the old ones. New theories take us closer to the 'truth'. Gradually, we approach a 'true' understanding of a concept or phenomenon, but we never really dispose of the older theories – they move into the background as newer ones that offer better explanations take their place.

Kuhn's approach is different. He saw science as working in two distinct phases, which he called normal and revolutionary. In normal science, scientists work on puzzle-solving activities, gradually building up solutions to problems, like the way a crossword puzzle-solver approaches clues. Scientists are taught the theories, beliefs and practices shared by the community, in the same way that a crossword puzzle-solver becomes used to a particular type of puzzle, such as cryptic, quick or general knowledge. Kuhn applied the term paradigm to describe the network or framework surrounding normal science activities. Within normal science, anomalies may arise. These are observations that don't immediately fit the paradigm. Some are resolved by further work, modification of existing theories, development of new pieces of equipment, or realising that an error was made. Other anomalies are set aside as inexplicable. Eventually, anomalies arise that undermine the existing framework so significantly that science enters a revolutionary phase in which competition occurs among theories to establish a new paradigm. Science undergoes a paradigm shift, the new paradigm generally offering greater puzzle-solving power, including resolution of the troublesome anomalies.

Kuhn's ideas can be illustrated using the 'white solids' example described on page 14. 'All white solids are crystalline' is a simple paradigm (in reality, a paradigm comprises more than one theory). The theory offers some puzzle-solving power, allowing scientists to carry out experiments. They would find compounds that do not fit the theory. These can be set aside while normal science continues, or we could modify the theory to apply under certain conditions of temperature and pressure. Over time, evidence undermines the theory significantly, as so many crystalline solids are found that are not white, and many white solids are found not to be crystalline. This leads to the statement 'all white solids are *not* crystalline'. This is a serious anomaly, incompatible with the overriding paradigm. 'Revolutionary science' occurs while scientists sort out a new one, such as 'some white solids are crystalline' and/or 'white solids may be non-crystalline or crystalline'. Eventually, science settles down to normal puzzle-solving again, but under a new paradigm.

Kuhn saw revolutions as rare events resulting in significant change. Normal science is not dramatic, but results in steady accumulation of knowledge. His ideas provide a powerful way of understanding how change comes about in science, an aspect absent from both Bacon's and Popper's work.

Faults with Kuhn's scientific revolutions

Some criticisms of Kuhn's ideas are as follows.

♦ Kuhn doesn't say if there is a difference between science that is part of an overruling paradigm and science that is 'normal'. This means there is no consistent definition about what a paradigm shift really looks like. What is perceived as a paradigm shift by some people is not regarded as such by others – they would argue that a change is just normal science.
♦ Paradigm shifts can occur without revolution. For example, finding that DNA has a double helix structure resulted from inspired insight by scientists Crick and Watson during a period of normal science, yet this resulted in the molecular genetics revolution. Kuhn does not include insightful science in normal science.
♦ Some theories describe the same phenomena, for example, Einstein and Newton both use the concept 'mass', but with different meanings. Kuhn argues that we can't say 'Einstein's theory is an improvement on Newton's' because they perceived things differently based on the beliefs and practices of their two eras, so these can't be compared. He says they are incommensurable – the two theories look at the same issue from different perspectives. Each theory came into being in a different era, so setting them against each other is not relevant. Others disagree with Kuhn and say that Einstein's theory simply is closer to the truth than Newton's. This problem has not yet been resolved. In practice, both theories are still in use, but in different circumstances. We haven't really rejected Newton's theories, so a paradigm shift cannot really have occurred.

Despite the criticisms, Kuhn's work has been highly influential, contributing to our understanding of the process of change. His ideas contrast with Popper's by describing scientists' actual behaviour, rather than saying what scientists should do. For example, Kuhn proposes that scientists try as hard as possible to maintain their theories, ignoring anomalies and/or making modifications to sustain a paradigm, until the drive for change becomes irresistible. Popper suggests that a scientist should reject a theory as soon as evidence is produced to contradict it. Kuhn says this doesn't happen in practice. Nevertheless, philosophers have not fully accepted Kuhn's ideas, as if he stimulated a revolution but did not provide a new paradigm to fill the void. By the end of the 1980s, a move back to Popper's views occurred. Although Kuhn's ideas are significant, the poor definition of what we could call the paradigm concept leads to the possibility that, in the long term, his philosophy of science will be less enduring than that of Popper.

◆ *Imre Lakatos – research programmes*

Box 1.4 Imre Lakatos (1922–94)

Imre Lakatos was born in Debrecen, Hungary. His surname at birth was Lipschitz. As he grew up, Lakatos's life became dominated by surviving Nazi persecution. His mother and grandmother died in Auschwitz, but he avoided being sent to the gas chambers by taking a Hungarian surname, becoming Imre Molnár. During the war years, Lakatos studied at the University of Debrecen, graduating in 1944 with a degree in mathematics, physics and philosophy. He became an active communist, and it is said that in keeping with his views he took the working class surname Lakatos, meaning 'locksmith'. For the next few years, Lakatos's career as a rising academic was dictated by challenges arising from the political situation. Post-war Hungary became a communist country allied with Stalin's Russia. In this period, Lakatos studied in Budapest in Romania and at Moscow State University, returning to Hungary in 1947 to work at the Ministry of Education. Being on the 'correct' side of the communist party was important – Lakatos's views were perceived as 'revisionist', and not in line with current thinking. As a result he was imprisoned from 1950–53 in a Stalinist jail. On his release, a friend helped him find work translating mathematics books into Hungarian. On 1 November 1956, the Hungarian uprising against the ruling Russian regime occurred. The swift invasion by Russia two days later generated chaos, with arrests and 'disappearances'. Lakatos fled to Vienna and found his way to England.

Lakatos registered as a postgraduate at the University of Cambridge, completing his doctoral degree on mathematical philosophy in 1961. In 1960, shortly before his doctorate was complete, he was appointed as a lecturer at the London School of Economics, joining Karl Popper. Despite living in the UK for many years, Lakatos never took British citizenship, so remained a stateless person. He died at the age of 51 from a brain haemorrhage.

Lakatos's contribution to science philosophy tried to reconcile Popper's and Kuhn's views. He described 'research programmes', a way of seeing progress in science rationally, taking into account the historical record of former theories. A research programme comprises a set of theories and practices sharing a common idea that Lakatos called the 'hard core'. A research programme can be progressive, generating new theories and novel insights; or degenerative, not growing and developing.

Lakatos proposed that rather than regarding a theory as an absolute statement, we should think of it as a succession of theories that has changed over time, along with the development of experimental techniques. The theories may share an unchanging idea that forms the hard core. The collection of theories, some current, others older, constitutes a research programme. Scientists work in the programme to protect the core from falsification. This means developing protection in the form of what Lakatos terms 'auxiliary hypotheses'. These act as a 'belt', holding up the core idea. The auxiliary hypotheses could be adjusted as scientists worked, for example, on resolving anomalies and developing new ideas. Popper's theory would say that this is not acceptable, because if evidence indicated that a hypothesis was false, this should be rejected. Lakatos chose a different line, saying that adjusting the protective belt was not a bad thing. Instead, adjustment would make comparisons possible between different research programmes with the same core. One might be developing new theories, generating novel discoveries, new experimental techniques, more accurate predictions, and so on, so could be described as progressive. Another, not leading to the discovery of new information, and/or with a weak protective belt, would be degenerative.

We can adapt the 'all white solids are crystalline' theory used earlier to illustrate these points. The hard core idea, 'white solids have crystalline characteristics', can be supported by two different sets of auxiliary hypotheses: one could be our original, that 'all white solids are crystalline'; another, more developed, states 'white solids tested at room temperature and pressure' and 'white solids can be crystallised from saturated solutions'. The second could lead to experiments in which temperature and pressure varied, perhaps developing new techniques for studying solids. The results may lead to further statements or hypotheses that could be added to the protective belt, such as 'crystallinity depends on regular arrangements of particles' and 'crystalline properties change under different conditions of temperature and pressure'. This is an example of a progressive research programme. The alternative, our original, is degenerative, as experiments lead only to evidence that cannot be supported by new hypotheses.

◆ *Comparing Lakatos, Popper and Kuhn*

To add more depth to our understanding of how science works, we compare Lakatos's ideas with those of Popper and Kuhn.

Popper's emphasis is on falsification; scientists behave irrationally if they hold on to theories to which, as he put it 'nature shouts NO'. Kuhn, on the other hand, claims this is exactly what scientists do – they modify theories to account for anomalies, throwing them out entirely only when forced. Lakatos takes the middle ground, saying, 'It is not that we propose a theory and Nature may shout NO, rather we propose a maze of theories and Nature may shout INCONSISTENT' (Lakatos and Musgrave, 1970, p. 130). Using research programmes, a core can be retained, but auxiliary hypotheses altered. The ability to adjust the protective belt is a distinguishing feature of a progressive research programme. A degenerative one risks being falsified, like our original 'white solids' theory, and superseded by a better set of proposals. Preferring a new research programme is Lakatos's way of explaining significant change in scientific thinking; he believes this is what happens during the periods Kuhn terms revolutionary science. Using these sorts of argument, Lakatos was attempting both to appease Popper (not always easy, given his temperament) by including falsification in his proposals, and to indicate how changes occur, thus adapting some of Kuhn's ideas. Lakatos's early death prevented his fully developing these proposals – he apparently had much work in mind at the time he died. We are left with a powerful way of perceiving science and scientific progress.

◆ *Paul Feyerabend – against method*

Box 1.5 Paul Feyerabend (1924–94)

Paul Karl Feyerabend was born in Vienna. His father was a civil servant and his mother a seamstress. Like Lakatos, his future friend, Feyerabend's early life was dominated by the Nazi regime, but as a non-Jew he was on the other side. He was a talented singer, taking singing lessons for much of his life. In 1938 Austria and Germany reunited, subjecting Austrians to Nazi rule. Aged 16, Feyerabend was inducted into the Nazi work service, the Arbeitsdienst, and later was drafted into the German Army, volunteering for officer training, in part, it is believed, to avoid front-line fighting and ensure survival. Despite hopes of avoiding conflict, Feyerabend's unit was sent to fight the advancing Russian army. He was awarded the Iron Cross, a high

honour, for bravery, and promoted. In the war's closing months, while serving in Poland, Feyerabend was wounded. A bullet hit his spine, causing temporary paralysis and permanent damage that resulted in his walking with a stick. Post-war, Feyerabend stayed in Germany studying singing and stage management, returning to Vienna in 1947 to study history and sociology at university. He changed to physics and developed interests in philosophy, attending a meeting in 1948 at which he met Karl Popper. Feyerabend completed a doctorate degree in philosophy in 1951 for a thesis on 'basic statements'. He was awarded a post-doctoral scholarship to study in England, to work with the famous philosopher Ludwig Wittgenstein, but Wittgenstein died. Instead, Feyerabend chose Karl Popper as his supervisor; like Popper and Lakatos, he came to the London School of Economics.

Feyerabend was something of a maverick. In the 1950s, his roving spirit took him to Vienna, Bristol, and finally to Berkeley in California, where he settled, becoming an American citizen in 1959. Even then,

Feyerabend took up visiting professorships around the world, working and publishing continually on philosophical problems and issues. He had a reputation for never taking academic duties seriously, once refusing an office as this allowed him to avoid office-based duties and, while at Berkeley, giving all students an A grade regardless of their work quality, doubtless to save himself the trouble of doing any marking. He and Lakatos were great friends: Feyerabend was badly affected by Lakatos's early death. From 1989 he was based mainly in Zurich, where he died in 1994 from an inoperable brain tumour.

Feyerabend wrote *Against Method* (1975), in which he argues there is no such thing as one scientific method; scientists are simply opportunists who use any possible method to solve problems and generate new ideas, ignorant of any theoretical structures suggesting how things should be done.

So far we have summarised the views of philosophers who each propose a specific way of thinking about science, described in technical language. Feyerabend's proposal is different. He claims there is no one scientific method explaining how science works, or how scientists should or do behave. He could see no rules that apply consistently to explain either the growth of scientific knowledge or how science progresses. Feyerabend is described as an 'epistemological anarchist'; essentially, anything goes. He saw the history of science as so complex that 'anything goes' was the only generally acceptable methodology, which of course is not a theory at all. Feyerabend cited Galileo in his favour, pointing out that the great scientist was not so much a scientific hero as a skilled master of rhetoric and propaganda, using tricks to promote his new, Sun-centred view of the Solar System. In saying this, Feyerabend placed greater emphasis on non-scientific factors dictating scientific revolutions. By this he meant that personalities, aesthetic criteria and social factors influence the direction and timing of changes in scientific thinking just as much as, if not more than, the development of scientific knowledge itself. Feyerabend wanted to:

> free people from the tyranny of philosophical obfuscators and abstract concepts such as 'truth', 'reality' or 'objectivity' which narrow people's vision and ways of being in the world. (Lakatos and Musgrave, 1970, p. 179)

Feyerabend's view, unsurprisingly given this statement, was that formal theories such as empiricism (the belief that knowledge derives from experience), together with Popper's falsificationism, inhibit scientific progress by placing tight conditions on what constitutes a theory. He saw Lakatos's research programmes as a more sophisticated version of his own ideas, permitting more flexibility about what is good science. He suggested that research programmes could just be 'epistemological anarchy' in disguise. So there is no point illustrating Feyerabend's work using the 'white solids' example – in fact, we could best illustrate his thinking by offering a range of suggestions as to how the theory may develop, as he would claim 'anything goes'.

Feyerabend's ideas were heavily criticised. Interestingly, he could not take this, becoming very depressed by the poor reviews received by *Against Method*. He failed to see that criticism was unavoidable, as his book effectively poured scorn on almost everyone else's work. Eventually, Feyerabend realised that he had undermined science's privileged position in Western culture as a standard-bearer for how knowledge develops: if there is no scientific method, it was argued that science cannot be justified as the best way of acquiring knowledge. If non-scientific factors have a big influence on progress, then results cannot necessarily be believed to represent excellence, because they can depend as much on showmanship, nepotism and money as on academic rigour. Feyerabend makes us sceptical, arguing that science threatens democracy, and consequently should be placed under firm control – so-called science 'experts' should be trusted only if they are controlled by juries of democratically elected lay people.

Since his death, Feyerabend has, to some extent, gained respect as a 'cultural relativist', someone who believes that a human being's actions and beliefs should be interpreted in terms of the person's culture. This built on his criticism of science itself as, objectively, being no better than subjects such as astrology, voodoo and alternative medicine, which are regarded by many as unreliable and disreputable. Feyerabend's 'anything goes' principle allows each a place in culture, based on the actions and beliefs of their proponents. Although today people might agree there is no one 'scientific method', and that science knowledge develops in various ways, its unlikely, for example, that a trained scientist would credit astrology as a subject on an equal footing with his/her own. To do so would put science on a par with superstition, taking the subject back to the mid-nineteenth century, where this chapter started.

1.4 Summary and key points

You may feel having reached the end of a 'heavy' chapter on science philosophy that you are none the wiser. We have not described how science works, but instead reported the views of five dead male philosophers, and what relevance are they? The philosophers provide ideas about how they think science should work 'in principle'. Popper tries to tell scientists what they should do; Kuhn tries to describe what scientists actually do in practice. Both give principles, or representations of science. None of the philosophies represent real science – all have their strengths and weaknesses. The Card Exchange activity reflects this variation - what do you defend as science? And why do you defend this? A theoretical physicist may defend different statements from a marine biologist or a medicinal chemist. But all are scientists, each working from a different standpoint.

The problem is that, in the UK at least, school science (as distinct from 'real world' science) has, over the last twenty years tended to focus one principle alone – that of scientific method based on developing an understanding of variables, hypotheses and inferences. Science teaching has adopted this successfully, through investigations. 'How science works' offers a chance to break away from this dogma, showing science 'warts and all'. That is what the rest of the book attempts. But this is a challenge – first because it relies on teachers' abilities to adopt different viewpoints that don't necessarily fit with their way of thinking about science and second, because anyone who has been teaching for a few years will have to change their classroom practice, which is never easy. Hence the purpose of this chapter - we don't suggest teachers stand in front of students and say 'This is an example of Kuhn's philosophy', but to have the variety of philosophies for science in mind when teaching – to know that there is no one way of approaching science correctly. Guy Claxton writes that theories are like tools – they are useful for specific purposes, but there is no point using a hammer when you really need a screwdriver.

1.5 References and resources

Chalmers, A. (1982) What Is This Thing Called Science? (2nd edn). Milton Keynes: Open University Press.

Claxton, G (1991) *Educating the inquiring mind: the challenge for school science*. Hemel Hempstead: Harvester Wheatsheaf.

Cobern, W.W. and Loving, C.C. (1998) The Card Exchange: Introducing the philosophy of science. In: *The Nature of Science in Science Education: Rationales and Strategies*, edited by William F. McComas. Dordrecht, the Netherlands: Kluwer Academic.

Feyerabend, P. (1975) *Against Method*. London: New Left Books (now Verso).

Feyerabend, P. (1993) *Against Method* (3rd edn). London: Verso.

Hacking, I. (ed.) (1981) *Scientific Revolutions*. Oxford: Oxford University Press.

Kuhn, T. (1962) *The Structure of Scientific Revolutions*. Chicago, IL, USA: University of Chicago Press.

Kuhn, T. (1970) *The Structure of Scientific Revolutions* (2nd edn, enlarged). Chicago, IL, USA: University of Chicago Press.

Lakatos, I. and Musgrave, A. (1970) *Criticism and the Growth of Knowledge*. Cambridge: Cambridge University Press.

Lederman, N. and Abd-El-Khalick, F. (1998) Avoiding de-natured science: activities that promote understandings of the nature of science. In: *The Nature of Science in Science Education: Rationales and Strategies* (edited by William F. McComas). Dordrecht, the Netherlands: Kluwer Academic.

McComas, W.F. (ed.) (1998) *The Nature of Science in Science Education: Rationales and Strategies*. Dordrecht, the Netherlands: Kluwer Academic.

Popper, K.R. (1959) *The Logic of Scientific Discovery*. London: Hutchinson Education.

Jenkins, E. (2007) *School science: a questionable construct?* Journal of Curriculum Studies 39 (3): 265–282

Williams, J. (2007) *Do we know how science works? A brief history of the scientific method* School Science Review 89 (327): 119–124

Wolpert, L. (1998) *The unnatural nature of science*. Harvard, USA : Harvard University Press

Crime Scene Investigation (CSI): www.cbs.com/primetime/csi – this website supports the TV programme with background information about the kinds of forensic work, giving some good opportunities for discussions on the nature of science using topical material.

Intute: www.intute.ac.uk/artsandhumanities/cgi-bin/browse.pl?id=200785 – a database of resources selected, evaluated and described by subject specialists, drawn mainly from university materials. The website lists sources introducing philosophy of science, giving links to the University of Cambridge among others. The resources are for teachers who want to know more.

2 | *Scientific developments*

2.1 Why do you need this chapter?

This chapter aims to:

♦ show how scientific discoveries are made in practice
♦ show ways in which science has contributed to our society
♦ outline general characteristics of scientific developments
♦ encourage thinking about how science may develop in future.

Students need to appreciate the extent to which science has contributed to great improvements in the overall quality of life in western cultures. We tend to take for granted things that were originally the subject of often intense scientific research and regarded as great progress for society. For example, anyone aged over about 40 can remember when space exploration was regarded as a fantastic novelty: as a child, TV programmes about the Apollo space missions, and particularly the Moon landings, were regarded as so momentous we were allowed to stay up late to watch. Today, the International Space Station is in permanent orbit and space shuttles are in regular use, but the idea of them using valuable airtime seems crazy. Similarly, the structure of DNA was discovered only in 1953 – only in the middle of the last century. Now, gene technology features in school science courses, while the double helix structure of DNA is simply a minor feature in the background. The relentless progress of scientific knowledge to date is clear.

In this chapter, we get to the heart of how scientific discoveries such as these are made. The activities encourage students to think about the role of evidence and experiments, and how jumps in understanding occur. We also try to get across how scientists think in order to make discoveries – being curious, and applying logic and reason.

Finally, it is important to ask if science can continue to contribute to society in the way it has to date. Every day we read of new scientific discoveries being made around the world. Some will have life-changing consequences for many of us as we age, seek jobs, drive cars, buy houses, have children, become ill, and so on. What scientific discoveries being made today might be taken for granted in the future? Will discoveries continue to be made at the same rate? Have all the really big questions been answered?

We provide four activities along with background material. The first activity uses the example of the northern lights (aurora borealis) to show how a scientific explanation for a natural phenomenon can be achieved. The next two activities have medical themes. The first of these is a data analysis exercise illustrating how medicine as a field has contributed to significant improvements in the health and wellbeing of many people. In the third activity we use a specific example, the discovery of how the stomach functions, to illustrate how even simple experiments can have large consequences for our understanding. The fourth activity encourages students to think about questions that science has not yet answered. This is a research-based task likely to stimulate a good discussion.

2.2 Activities

◆ *What causes the northern lights?*

Time required: about 25 minutes
NC link: 1b, c; 2d

Learning outcomes

- ◆ To find out the jumps in understanding that led to the correct explanation.
- ◆ To recognise the evidence collected and used by scientists in making the jumps.
- ◆ To explain how the evidence supported the new understanding.
- ◆ To consider if evidence for the new theory is reliable.

Background

This activity uses the explanation for the northern lights as an example of a scientific discovery that can be traced from myths and folklore. Evidence is presented that helps students see the jumps in understanding.

Requirements: northern lights fact sheet, timeline and task sheet, provided on the CD.

Starter activity

Introduce the topic by discussing the notion of myths and legends. Students may know myths and legends associated with the weather, for example:

- red sky at night, shepherd's delight
- red sky in the morning, sailors' warning
- rain on St Swithin's day (15 July) brings 40 days of rain.

You could also discuss any of the following.

- comets – fire in the sky; a curse; a bringer of good luck; a source of poison.
- volcanoes – powered by the god Vulcan in Roman mythology; created by gods in memory of the Aztec Popoca in Mexico; created by Pélé the goddess of fire in Hawaii.
- eclipses – caused by an invisible dragon eating the Sun; a warning that something bad will happen.

Students may discuss:

- what do they notice about these ideas?
- where do they come from?
- why do people have these ideas?
- do we think like this today? If so, why / why not?

Main activity

A short video of northern lights in Alaska is available at www.northern-lights.no and may help set the scene for this activity.

The task involves organising the material provided to illustrate the timeline on finding the cause of the aurora. Students discuss the evidence and identify the key jumps leading to the scientist Kristian Birkeland's explanation.

They may be surprised to find out that electrons (tiny particles) producing the aurora come from the Sun. This was a difficult point to accept, even at the time. Discuss with students whether the evidence for this was reliable – the graph linking the sunspots to the northern lights is good for this point. Also note that evidence confirming the notion was obtained independently only years later, in the 1950s and 1960s, using satellites. This indicates that scientists sometimes have correct ideas, but cannot always prove them.

Plenary discussion

The questions on the task sheet can be used in a plenary discussion. Draw out these points:

- scientists rely on using evidence from different experiments to arrive at an explanation
- scientists don't automatically accept a new explanation – they are sceptical
- scientists need reliable evidence to change their mind
- evidence supporting a new theory may be produced years later
- some people don't change their mind, but believe the old-fashioned views.

◆ *Declining death, improving health*

Time required: about 60 minutes
NC link: 3a, b, c

Learning outcomes

- To analyse data relating to declining child death rates in the UK.
- To connect the decline in child death to improvements in health provision.
- To realise that scientific discoveries in medicine were major contributors.

Background

This activity looks at how improvements in health provision have contributed to reducing the number of people dying and to increasing our life expectancy. Students are encouraged to use the timeline of medical developments (on the CD) as qualitative evidence to help explain quantitative data showing the reduction in the death rate.

Starter activity

Show students the graph of declining mortality in the UK during the twentieth century (on the CD).

1. Ask students to describe what the graph is saying.
2. Ask students to raise questions about the information shown on the graph, for example:
   a) What caused the decline?
   b) Why are there spikes in certain years?
   c) The drop from 1900 to 1950 is bigger than that from 1950 to 2000. Explain why.
   d) What other evidence would be needed to support the information in the graph?

Main activity

Requirements: timeline showing medical developments; fact sheet showing numbers dying of infectious diseases; graph (on the CD) showing reduction in child death rate 1901–2000; additional online resources (see pages 55–57).

Teaching points

Students are asked to develop an argument to explain the changes in death rate and causes of death that occurred during the twentieth century in the UK, using the information provided and by carrying out additional research. Clues are provided in the timeline and the fact sheet showing the extent of improvement in health during the twentieth century, achieved largely through consistent development of new medicines, vaccines and better diagnosis. Students' arguments must be based on evidence from different sources, use technical language, and present a conclusion.

♦ Students could draw on key skills using ICT in preparing a presentation.
♦ Assessment for learning through peer review on agreed criteria is also possible.

This is a good task to differentiate by ability. Groups of students could be asked to research various questions, such as the following (organised broadly in order of difficulty).

♦ What caused the major decline in death rate?
A description should be based on a major decline in infectious diseases due to improved hygiene, vaccination, antibiotics and other drugs. Students could also explore which factor was the biggest contributor.
♦ What caused the spikes we see in the lines on the graph?
Spikes during the years of the two World Wars represent deaths in battle and an increase in suicides; the General Strike in the 1920s also created a spike; the major influenza epidemic in 1919 also caused a spike.
♦ Women's death rates are lower. Why is this?
Men traditionally had heavy industry labouring jobs that were more dangerous and brought greater risk of work-related illness, e.g. mining, factory work, ship-building; they also fought in the World Wars. Men do not go to doctors and are generally less aware of their health than women. More men than women smoke and drink heavily.
♦ Why can the death rate only be reduced, not eliminated?
Some illnesses have not changed much in frequency, e.g. cancers, heart disease, other smoking-related diseases, diabetes,

mental illness; other illnesses, such as multiple sclerosis, Parkinson's disease and Alzheimer's disease, are still incurable. The body does age, and decline in functions is only to be expected. We will all die a natural death eventually unless we are killed first by something else! Accidents still happen. Research on life expectancy rates may be worthwhile here.

♦ What fatal diseases in the twenty-first century have increased in frequency since 1901?
Some death rates from certain illnesses have increased, e.g. drug abuse, alcohol-related illness, heart disease, smoking-related illnesses, HIV-AIDS, while others are returning, e.g. tuberculosis. The main changes have occurred in child health. In 1901 over half of deaths were of people aged under 45, compared with fewer than 4% in 2006.

Plenary discussion

This could be led by groups of students presenting their findings and conclusions. Overall, points to draw out are:

♦ evidence from a range of sources can be used to support a conclusion
♦ patterns in data need to be explained – this can be on a large scale (the overall decline) and a small scale (spikes in the graphs)
♦ big changes in society come about through improvements in many factors – science makes contributions, but does not solve everything.

♦ *A medical discovery – how does the stomach work?*

Time required: about 40 minutes
NC link: 1a, b, c; 2a, b

Learning outcomes

♦ To use an example of direct experimentation on the human body as a context for collection of data.
♦ To interpret the data as a test for a hypothesis.
♦ To show that ideas can be changed by direct experiment.
♦ To consider the reliability of experimental evidence.

Background

This activity illustrates how doctors took scientific approaches to finding out how the body works. The activity is a comprehension exercise based on original information provided by William Beaumont, an American doctor working in the nineteenth century.

Requirements: fact sheet and question sheet (provided on the CD).

Starter activity

Using an outline of the body as a basis, invite students to suggest where they think the body organs are. This could be done on a whiteboard as a whole-class activity, with individuals coming to the board to draw in turn, or each student could complete their own body, making comparisons afterwards.

Body organs to locate – heart, lungs, kidneys, liver, stomach, small intestine, colon, pancreas.

Compare students' suggestions with Figure 2.1.

Figure 2.1 *The main body organs*

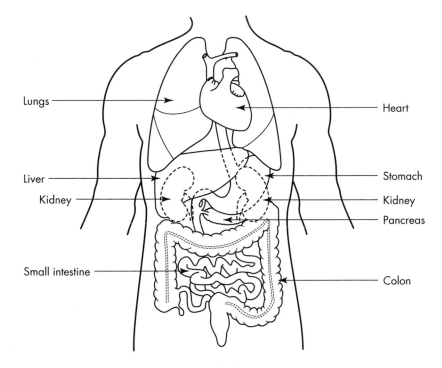

Questions like these may be helpful:

♦ which where hardest to locate?
♦ why was this?
♦ what evidence might we need in order to find out where the organs are?
♦ how did doctors find out where the organs were before X-rays and other diagnostic instruments were invented?

Main activity

This comprehension exercise asks students to use the information provided to show how a doctor, William Beaumont, first discovered how the stomach works. His starting point, primitive debate about the role of the stomach, is provided. Students work from some of Beaumont's original findings to establish the function. This is a retrospective exercise, as we now know what the stomach does, but the task is rather like the starter activity in which students had to think about where the body organs were, with only limited information: doctors worked with a 'black box' (see Chapter 1, page 7) using small amounts of information, some of which may have been wrong, to guide their actions. Students can imagine what it must have been like to be a curious doctor presented with the opportunity to investigate.

Possible answers to the questions on the sheet are as follows.

1. People felt hunger and stomach rumbling, but did not connect this with the brain – the stomach seemed to do this by itself.
   Everyone produced faeces – this could be bad food rejected by the stomach. The 'unclean' image could also come from the association with faeces production.
   People will have been ill with vomiting at various times, realising this came from the stomach. Hence the idea of keeping the stomach healthy.
   The origin of the notion of fire in the liver is uncertain. This could be because of associated illnesses showing the importance of the liver, or medical books saying the liver was very important in the body, or perhaps the body felt hottest around the liver.

2. All these statements can be regarded as correct. However, they are very limited.

3. Possible hypotheses:
   Does food disappear in the stomach?
   Which foods disappear most quickly?
   Does the stomach sort food?
   Does the stomach grind, cook or ferment food?

4. He lowered samples of food into the hole in Alexis St Martin's stomach. He found that food disappeared gradually. He took samples of gastric juice, finding that it could dissolve food, but did not work as well when cold.

5. This depends on the hypothesis. Linking with the hypotheses above (question 3):
   yes
   see text

no

no

6. This work showed that food dissolves in the stomach. It isn't cooked, fermented or ground up, or sorted out. The stomach dissolves all food, but takes different amounts of time to do this. No-one had known this before.

7. Depends on students' answers to question 1.

Plenary discussion

Points to draw out in reviewing the activity:

◆ the nature of the evidence that Dr Beaumont collected – this relied on one patient only, but he collected it over a long period of time

◆ his experiments produced primary source data that were reliable

◆ Beaumont's work solved a puzzle about the stomach that had existed for many years.

◆ *What do scientists know? What remains to be found out?*

Time required: about 50 minutes for option 1 and 30 minutes for option 2 (see page 40).

NC link: 1d; 4b, c

Learning outcomes

◆ To realise there are questions that science cannot answer.

◆ To realise that science can change over time – questions that can't be answered today may be answerable in the future.

◆ To realise that there are questions science cannot address – these are issues for society to resolve.

◆ To realise that some questions raise ethical issues.

Background

Students are presented with different images, each representing an aspect of our world. For each image they are asked to say what scientists already know, and what questions they would like to ask. This could be done as an open-ended task involving extra research, or as a relatively short activity using the images alone. The activity will distinguish between questions that science can or cannot answer, as well as those that are not for science to address.

Requirements: images and questions (provided on the CD).

Starter activity

This lesson could be introduced by asking students to consider questions that may have surprising or controversial answers.

♦ Why do some people believe in ghosts? What explanations are there for ghosts?
♦ What would happen if the Sun didn't rise tomorrow morning?
♦ Why do we buy birthday cards and presents for people?
♦ Why do people take astrology seriously?

The point is to not accept a yes/no answer, but to open students' minds to possibilities. Whatever questions are asked, try to tap into basic assumptions, things that we don't normally question. Raise students' curiosity and stimulate their thinking.

Main activity

Divide the class into groups of about three – 10 images are provided. Groups could swap images after a fixed time. More images could be added.

The images are graded, permitting differentiation.

Easy

♦ Earth – what can we do to prevent global warming? And save the Earth?
♦ Floods – how can we control the effects of climate change?
♦ Car – what will we use to replace fossil fuels?

Medium

♦ Periodic Table – how many chemical elements can we make?
♦ Genes – can we make perfect people? Should we?
♦ Nanotechnology – how small can we go?

Difficult

♦ Brain – how do we think? What is consciousness?
♦ Particle physics – what is matter made of?
♦ Human embryo – how do body organs form from just a group of cells?
♦ Deep space – is there another universe?

For each image, students are asked to say:

♦ what scientists know in this area – this is limited to what students themselves know
♦ what questions scientists still have to answer.

Here are two suggestions for running this activity:

♦ give each group one image, allow research time, then in the plenary discussion allow either all groups or selected groups to present their findings
♦ give each group one image, brainstorm questions, and then change – the plenary discussion will be more of an overview of the images, whereas allowing research time will enable issues to be considered in greater depth.

Plenary discussion

Make sure students distinguish between questions that:

♦ are legitimate for scientific investigation
♦ are for society to decide
♦ cannot be answered at the moment – Why not? Might these be answerable in the future?

Discuss whether students think science is coming to an end – what would be needed in order to answer the scientific questions? Can they be answered? Might they be answered in the future? See page 53 for a table of contrasting views.

2.3 Background information

♦ *General characteristics of scientific developments*

Many scientific developments have arisen through the following steps.

♦ Mythology and folklore (a mystical era) – the period when people attempt to make sense of observations and experiences without a formal knowledge base.
♦ Pre-science – when scientists begin to study the phenomenon, or work on an idea, but there is no agreed theory. Theories compete to be the key idea that leads to a solution or discovery.
♦ An established paradigm phase – when scientists have agreed on a theoretical basis for further work.
♦ Finally, a discovery is made, or a theory proposed that provides strong evidence for a final, or at least more rigorous, explanation or solution.

These stages broadly follow the philosophy of science suggested by Thomas Kuhn (see Chapter 1, page 18). His approach is useful in tracing how scientific developments occur.

Mythology and folklore represent humans' instinctive desire to understand the world around them in the absence of formal knowledge. In the past, mythology and folklore provided scientists with ideas for research. This no longer occurs in Western culture, as such beliefs have been mainly replaced by understanding based on scientific knowledge. However, some people still choose to believe in explanations or events based on informal knowledge: 'old wives' tales', astrology, religious faith healing and other alternative approaches remain well known.

The pre-science stage occurs when rational explanations are sought. This stage can be blurred with folklore as the rational approach struggles for clarity and acceptance. In pre-science, a wide range of theories and ideas are worked on, rather than progress being made on a few.

A third stage results when ideas are narrowed down, as scientists begin to agree about explanations for a phenomenon. At this point, the area of science develops paradigms and advances, contributing to our understanding and knowledge. A helpful image is to picture scientists building the same tower, rather than each working on their own, as in pre-science. Through common effort, a stronger, better tower is built, with additions and refinements being made with time. Today, all areas of science operate within paradigms, even if these continuously develop and change.

Eventually, an explanation may be reached that is likely to stand the test of time. Some are more finite than others: for example, 'the Earth is nearly spherical' (an oblate spheroid, to be precise) contrasts with the early myth, 'the Earth is flat'. The statement 'matter is made of tiny particles' cannot be challenged, and contrasts with 'matter is made of earth, wind, water or fire'. The ability of scientists to come up with the 'truth' means science is, perhaps, a victim of its own success. Making discoveries leaves fewer to be made. Applied science will always be able to come up with something new – but the possibility exists that pure science will run out of major discoveries.

◆ *The northern lights (aurora borealis)*

The northern lights appear around the magnetic north and south poles (in the southern hemisphere the phenomenon is called the southern lights, or aurora australis). They are seen as moving bands of colour in the night sky, often green and yellow, sometimes red and orange. The colours occur in repeating patterns as long, wavy lines, patches or rays streaming from a single point. The lights can be sufficiently bright to illuminate objects on the ground. The phenomenon is truly dramatic, startling and beautiful.

Mythology and folklore

Myths and folklore about the aurora developed in northern cultures over 2000 years, with many variants. Auroras are strongly associated with death – in the Viking period in Scandinavia, the lights were seen as spirits of dead maidens, while Greenland Inuits believed them to be dead souls playing football with walrus skulls. People believed that children could be killed by the lights reaching Earth. Another common myth was that the lights were a god, or represented spiritual influence. In Nordic mythology an aurora was a bridge called Bifrost (pronounced 'Beefrost') connecting the Earth to Asgard (pronounced 'Awsgard'), the world of the gods. In some areas of Scandinavia, Nordic people believed the aurora meant the gods were angry. Native Americans thought they could conjure up ghosts by whistling to the lights, or that the lights represented a great god's ability to light cold and dark areas of the Earth. A modern interpretation of a spiritual aurora myth is seen in the 2003 Disney film *Brother Bear*, in which a native North American Indian boy searches for the place where the lights touch the Earth in order to reclaim his brother's spirit. The movements of the lights inspired associations with dance: they were nicknamed 'the merry dancers' in Scotland; thought by Lapp people to be girls dancing round the fireplace; and seen by some American Indians as dancing gods. Many cultures in medieval times believed the aurora was an omen for bad events, such as war, famine or plagues.

In the southern hemisphere, the lights had little impact on human societies – we found no reference in Aboriginal and Maori cultures. Students may speculate as to why: the southern lights are seen over Antarctica mainly by penguins and, today, a few hardy scientists, because the Antarctic circle (the equivalent of the Arctic circle) lies south of Australia and New Zealand away from human habitation.

Box 2.1 provides a description of the northern lights written by Ernest Hawkes, an early twentieth-century polar explorer, based on information from north Canadian Eskimos. Note the images of Earth and sky.

Box 2.1 An Eskimo culture description of Earth and the northern lights

The ends of the land and sea are bounded by an immense abyss, over which a narrow and dangerous pathway leads to the heavenly regions. The sky is a great dome of hard material arched over the Earth. There is a hole in it through which the spirits pass to the true heavens. Only the spirits of those who have died a voluntary or violent death, and the raven, have been over this pathway. The spirits who live there light torches to guide the feet of new arrivals. This is the light of the aurora. They can be seen there feasting and playing football with a walrus skull.

The whistling crackling noise which sometimes accompanies the aurora is the voices of these spirits trying to communicate with the people of the Earth. They should always be answered in a whispering voice. Youths dance to the aurora. The heavenly spirits are called selamiut, 'sky-dwellers,' those who live in the sky.

Hawkes, E.W. (1916) *The Labrador Eskimo*. Ottawa: Geological Survey.

Two folklore stories were researched thoroughly by scientists. One was that the northern lights were caused by reflection of light from something on the ground or in the sea. Folklore suggested shoals of herring, while some Lapp people thought light reflected by lost reindeer or 'fire foxes' in the mountains was responsible. A second idea, as Hawkes suggests (Box 2.1) was that the lights made sounds. Most folklore and mythical beliefs died out as scientific evidence accumulated in favour of the lights being a natural phenomenon.

Pre-science

Scientific theories attempt rational explanations of phenomena. Among the earliest was proposed by the ancient Greek philosopher Aristotle, who recorded several auroras, explaining them as reactions between air and vapours from the ground. The *King's Mirror*, a book written in Norway around 1250 by an unknown author, presented three possible theories: two based on the principle of a flat Earth; the lights were caused by the Sun shining on the sky from beneath the horizon, or reflections of fire from the edge of the Earth. The third suggested that auroras were caused by ice.

More formal research began in the early eighteenth century, during the period known as the Enlightenment, when many medieval ideas were investigated and discarded. On 6 March 1716, particularly bright northern lights were seen over much of Europe, stimulating scientific interest. A number of theories competed, some proposed by eminent scientists of the day, including the British astronomer Edmond Halley, who suggested that the lights were caused by sulfur from the ground. He believed sulfur was released in earthquakes, but as he could not match observations of earthquakes with appearances of the northern lights, he suggested that 'magnetic fluid' was released around the Earth's poles. In competition was the American Benjamin Franklin's contribution, that electricity was involved, as electric charges were moved towards the poles in clouds, falling down to lower areas with snow. The high density of charge around the poles would create light.

Establishing a paradigm

During the nineteenth century, scientists agreed that the northern lights were an electrical phenomenon. This arose as evidence collected by various scientists all indicated that electric charge was involved. A key piece of information came from the Danish physicist Hans Christian Oersted (1777–1851), who showed that electric current caused a magnetic field. This principle explained why the northern lights affected a compass needle. Accompanying this was evidence from the Swedish physicist Anders Jonas Ångström (1814–74, pronounced 'Awngstrum'), that light from gases could form line spectra (angstrom units are named after him). Ångström showed that the northern lights were caused by a gas, and were not reflected sunlight. Thirdly, geophysics identified magnetic field lines around the Earth – these were found to follow the areas where the lights appear. Although none of these explained the cause of the lights directly, research became much more focused as a result. Scientists tried to recreate the conditions needed to produce the lights in the laboratory, combining electricity, magnetism and gases. Others tried to measure the heights of the light bands. New equipment and techniques developed as a result of these efforts.

Solving the puzzle

Another Scandinavian, the Norwegian scientist Kristian Birkeland (1867–1917), finally solved the mystery of the curious, dramatic, moving coloured bands. He set up a laboratory at the top of a mountain in a freezing Norwegian arctic winter, from which he observed and measured the phenomenon over several months. Birkeland established the height at which the lights occur – around 10 000 m (and higher) above the Earth's surface – and found that the lights were caused by electrons moving along magnetic field lines. Most startling of all, he proposed that the electrons came streaming to Earth directly from the Sun in a solar wind. As the electrons get caught by the Earth's magnetic field, they become focused at the poles, where they collide with atmospheric gas particles and cause the lights. Interaction with oxygen molecules causes the green and red colours; blue and deep red are caused by interaction with nitrogen molecules. The interactions form bands across the sky about 100 m wide, following magnetic field lines.

Figure 2.4
Kristian Birkeland and his magnetized terrella experiment

Birkeland's theory was dismissed initially, but was accepted once convincing evidence from laboratory experiments was produced. To collect this, Birkeland made a model Earth he called the terrella, a gas chamber with a magnetic field that produced miniature northern lights when bombarded with electrons. Reproducing such a special natural phenomenon must have been a fantastic sight and is a remarkable achievement – Birkeland was nominated for the Nobel Prize in Physics several times, but depression overtook him and he committed suicide before any great honour could be bestowed.

Research on the northern lights continues today, with observations being made both from Earth and space. A new observatory opened recently on Norway's northerly island of Spitsbergen to study the northern lights further.

◆ *Medicine*

Everyone needs medical care at some point, even if only at the extremes of birth and death. The quality and breadth of medical care have developed enormously in the past 150 years – today, if we are ill, we rely on the reasonable expectation of returning to health. Diseases that used to be deadly are now curable. The hunt is on to find treatments for conditions still regarded as incurable, including Parkinson's disease, multiple sclerosis, Alzheimer's disease, some cancers and diabetes. We review here some key medical developments, using the four headings suggested above as a guide.

Mythology and folklore

Every human culture has sought explanations and cures for illnesses and diseases. Many communities without formal knowledge still rely on traditional medicine based on magic, religious or spiritual ceremonies and herbal remedies. Magical cures often rely on driving out an evil spirit from the sick person's body by physical actions such as boring holes in the skull to allow the spirit to escape, drinking a potion made from sacred herbs, using an incantation, or a combination of these. For example, the Kaliai people of Papua New Guinea believe:

◆ there are intelligent spirits that exist inside and outside humans – angering or disrespecting these can cause illness and deformities (e.g. angering a bush spirit or masalai by cutting down a tree causes birth defects)
◆ a dead person can take a spirit away from a living person, causing illness
◆ a person's spirit can be trapped in a sorcerer's protective spell or kisinga, causing illness in the person until it is released.

In western cultures, 'old wives' tales' related to illness are common (see Box 2.2) and surprisingly persistent. Plants are given healing or mystical powers: mistletoe, for example, is regarded as a cure for many diseases, an antidote to poison and a bringer of good luck and fertility. Mandrake is associated with magic – it is said to scream when pulled up from the ground, and drinking a mandrake potion supposedly increases a woman's fertility.

Box 2.2 Old wives' tales about health and illness

<u>Myths about health and illness:</u>
Cut your hair on Good Friday to prevent headaches in the year to come.
If you catch a falling leaf on the first day of autumn, you will not catch a cold all winter.
An onion cut in half and placed under the bed of a sick person will draw off fever and poisons.
A red ribbon should be placed on a child who has been sick to keep the illness from returning.
The devil can enter your body when you sneeze. Having someone say, 'God bless you' drives the devil away.
Cats can steal the air from a baby's mouth.

<u>Other sayings, which are all false, include:</u>
If you touch a toad you will get warts.
Cracking knuckles causes arthritis.
Reading in dim light damages your eyes.
If you go outside with wet hair you'll catch cold.
Eating carrots improves your eyesight.
Feed a cold, starve a fever.
Wait an hour after eating before swimming.

Religion has long been a favoured source of treatment. Good health is seen as a god rewarding devotion, while ill health is a sign of a god's wrath, punishment or revenge. Various ways of pacifying angry gods have been invented, including prayer, confession, touching a religious artefact, fasting, offering payments or prayers at shrines and visiting faith healers. Members of religious communities continue to practise some of these methods today: in Christianity, the Sanctuary of Our Lady of Lourdes in France has received over 200 million visitors since its opening in 1860.

Pre-science

Even 2000 years ago, doctors in different cultures sought more rational explanations for illness and disease. Perhaps the most well known in Western culture is Hippocrates, the Greek physician writing around 500BC, now regarded by many as the father of medicine. He rejected religion and folklore as a basis for treating disease, believing that changes to diet, lifestyle and environment were more reliable. Hippocrates suggested that imbalance in four 'humours' caused illness. The humours – blood, black bile, yellow bile and phlegm – could be restored to balance by rest, good nourishment, and keeping the patient and the environment around him or her clean. Hippocrates emphasised the importance of observing patients carefully, writing down details. This began the principle of diagnosis and prognosis for future cases, skills used by doctors today. His Hippocratic Oath, a statement of ethical practice, is the basis for modern swearing-in ceremonies for newly trained doctors, particularly common in the USA. After Hippocrates, western medicine did not develop significantly until about AD200, when another Greek, Galen, began his work. Galen studied anatomy, making mistakes because he used animals rather than humans, and carried out surgery, even doing cataract operations on eyes using a needle. Galen's anatomical studies, supplemented by herbal medicines and myths and legends of popular culture, were the mainstay for doctors until the sixteenth century, when the Belgian Andreas Vesalius (1514–64) published his study of human anatomy.

Other approaches to medical practice were developed around the world – here are three.

- Ayurveda is the Indian science of living. This rigorous system of medicine was developed through collective practice by early Buddhists. An ayurvedic student would, over 7 years, be taught eight branches of medicine by a guru, as well as ten arts involved in making herbal and other preparations for use as treatments.
- Traditional Chinese medicine is based on Taoist, Buddhist and Confucian principles. Like Hippocrates's system, it starts from the premise that illnesses result when the body is out of balance. Treatment is based on a holistic or whole-body approach combining acupuncture, massage, food therapy, physical exercise, and medicines made from plants and animal body parts. A diagnostic system involving observation of body functions helps practitioners decide which treatments are most appropriate.
- Islamic medicine contributed significantly to medieval medicine through Muslim doctors, especially Ibn Sina, Al-Kindi and Abu al-Qasim. Ibn Sina, for example, discovered circulation of the blood in 1288, over 300 years before William Harvey did so in England. Abu al-Qasim wrote a 30-chapter medical book detailing surgical practice in a diverse range of fields, including dentistry and childbirth. Al-Kindi wrote many medical books that strongly influenced practice.

Establishment of paradigms

Medical developments were made in the seventeenth and eighteenth centuries by doctors who took a scientific approach to the body and diseases. Most new developments were at basic level, and some were erroneous.

Human dissection was a popular spectator sport for medical students, who gathered in high-tiered lecture theatres to watch. In 1628, William Harvey published his theory of blood circulation (doubtless unaware that the Islamic doctor Ibn Sina had already done so) with the heart at the centre of a double-pump system. John Hunter, a Scottish surgeon, was one of the first doctors to apply scientific experimentation methods to medicine. He lived in London, founding an anatomy school. One of Hunter's contributions was to explain how the lymphatic system drains excess fluid from body organs. This helped establish that dissection and investigation of the body could help develop surgical techniques and our understanding of body function. Surgery was still primitive – there were no anaesthetics, so patients were pinned, strapped down, deliberately knocked out, cooled, hypnotised or had their nerves compressed to reduce pain. Many died post-operatively due to wound infections.

Meanwhile, diagnosis and treatment of diseases remained a mystery. The theory of spontaneous generation suggested that living organisms appeared spontaneously in decaying organic matter, for example, maggots on bread. In the seventeenth century, Antonie van Leeuwenhoek (1632–1723) invented the microscope and saw bacteria. Applying the spontaneous generation theory meant that bacteria appeared spontaneously in tissue, causing infection. Another theory was that 'miasma' or bad air caused disease, particularly cholera and bubonic plague. Miasma was a poisonous gas coming from decomposing organisms.

Treatments were mainly based on herbal remedies, with few effective drugs – quinine (from cinchona bark) was used to treat fevers, while laudanum (a form of opium, a narcotic) gave pain relief. Blood-letting, proposed by Galen, was practised widely for almost any illness, on the belief that it was beneficial to health. This practice followed Hippocrates's theory of humours, that blood should be controlled.

The first scientifically correct, if simple, paradigm regarding disease treatment was the concept of cleanliness (suggested originally by Hippocrates). Disease travelled fast among people living close together in poor conditions, resulting in epidemics and many deaths. In the eighteenth century, Royal Navy Admiral John Jervis realised that more sailors survived long sea voyages when standards of cleanliness were high: the gundecks, where sailors worked and slept, were scrubbed clean with blocks of rock the size of a Bible, called holystones. Men's clothing was washed in salt water, the only known disinfectant, and hammocks were aired regularly. Cleanliness was formally identified as helping to prevent disease in 1847. The Austro-Hungarian doctor Ignaz Semmelweis (1818–65) found that if doctors attending mothers in childbirth washed their hands using a bleach solution, this significantly reduced the numbers dying from childbed fever. Joseph Lister (1827–1912) invented the carbolic spray for use during surgery. Carbolic acid is now known as phenol. He cleaned instruments with 5% phenol solution, sprayed the wound, and made sure nurses and doctors wore clean gloves. This antiseptic treatment helped prevent post-surgery infection, at that time responsible for killing about 50% of patients.

We highlight three other critical incidents that helped doctors understand disease.

♦ John Snow (1813–58) realised that around 89 deaths in a cholera outbreak in London in 1854 were connected – the victims drank water from a pump on Broad Street. The water came from a well that was close to a sewer. He had the pump handle removed, immediately reducing the spread of disease. This showed that diseases could be carried by water, not just air, contradicting the miasma theory.
♦ Edward Jenner (1749–1823) found that deliberately infecting a healthy child by scratching his skin and introducing a sample of pus from a cowpox blister protected the boy from getting potentially deadly smallpox. He invented vaccination.
♦ René Laennec (1781–1826) invented the stethoscope. He realised that sounds within the body could help diagnose diseases. The first stethoscope was a wooden tube, placed on the chest, for use with one ear only. The stethoscope was the first step towards using instruments to help doctors diagnose illnesses.

Solving the puzzles

On the surgical side, doctors continued to experiment with different operating procedures. Patients' survival and comfort were enhanced greatly by the development of reliable blood transfusions and anaesthesia. Blood-letting finally went out of fashion in the nineteenth century, as doctors realised that keeping blood in the body was more beneficial. Doctors began experimenting with small blood transfusions in the seventeenth century. The science developed to a higher level of safety when ABO blood types were found in the early twentieth century, followed by rhesus in 1937.

Anaesthesia enabled pain-free operations. The discovery that inhaling a drug before an operation would induce sleep and relieve pain was first demonstrated on 16 October 1846 by William Morton in Massachusetts General Hospital, Boston, USA, using diethyl ether, or 'ether'. The successful operation, in full view of an audience, removed a tumour from a man's jaw. This led to the development of anaesthetics, notably chloroform (1847), cocaine (1884), procaine (1904), epidurals (1921), thiopentone (1934), lignocaine (1946) and halothane (1956). Nitrous oxide became popular from the 1850s for tooth extractions and, eventually, for use in childbirth. Now new ethers are being made with anaesthetic properties.

In the late nineteenth century, the cause of many diseases was finally agreed to be bacteria, proposed as a 'germ theory' by Louis Pasteur (1822–95), following a series of careful experiments on broth. Pasteur, Ferdinand Cohn (1822–95) and Robert Koch (1843–1910) are together regarded as the founders of bacteriology. Cohn classified different types of bacteria and described the life cycle of bacillus, a rod-shaped variety. Koch found the organisms responsible for many diseases, including meningitis, tuberculosis, leprosy, tetanus, cholera and bubonic plague. Pasteur famously developed pasteurisation, a process to kill the bacteria that spoil milk.

Three other key developments have made major contributions to patient survival rates.

♦ The discovery in 1895 by Wilhelm Röntgen that X-rays could pass through human tissue and produce an image on a plate led to the development of new, non-invasive diagnostic techniques. Today we can expect to be scanned using magnetic resonance imaging (MRI) or computed tomography (CT) machines that give detailed images of body interiors.
♦ The discovery in 1928 by Alexander Fleming that a chemical from the penicillin mould could kill bacteria led to the development of antibiotics. This contributed to an explosion in the range of effective drugs available to treat diseases previously regarded as fatal.

♦ The announcement in 1953 by James Watson and Francis Crick, using data from Rosalind Franklin and Maurice Wilkins, that DNA, the material of which all our genes are made, has a double helix structure led to the development of molecular biology. This science has enabled analysis of genetic disorders and wide range of prenatal screening tests.

♦ *Discussion – the end of science?*

Science has contributed great advancements in all known areas of nature. Big ideas of science that form the basic principles for scientific activity include:

♦ theory of evolution
♦ Big Bang theory
♦ particle theory and the existence of sub-atomic particles
♦ quantum theory
♦ the Periodic Table of the chemical elements
♦ tectonic plate theory
♦ the double helix structure of DNA.

Within the framework these, scientists have made many other discoveries. Solving the puzzle of the northern lights is an example of pure science, a situation where a final answer is achieved to a problem. Medicine involves applied sciences, in which developments often rely on scientific discoveries being adapted for specific purposes. There has been discussion about whether pure science will eventually run out of possible discoveries, leaving only applications to be invented. The American science writer John Horgan (1996) takes this to extremes in his book *The End of Science*. Horgan likens science to exploring the Earth between the sixteenth and nineteenth centuries, when new continents and corners of the globe were found regularly. Finally, the whole Earth was mapped, each corner becoming known. He argues provocatively that scientists have successfully investigated all sectors of the natural world and, in their enthusiasm, have made all the big discoveries there are to be made. Similar points were made around 100 years ago, particularly about physics, as Box 2.3 shows.

Box 2.3 Contrasting views about the future for science

Physicists who thought all major discoveries in their science were made	Scientists who thought, or still think, science has many more discoveries to make
Max Planck, 1924 'When I began my physical studies [in Munich in 1874] and sought advice from my venerable teacher Philipp von Jolly ... he portrayed to me physics as a highly developed, almost fully matured science ... Possibly in one or another nook there would perhaps be a dust particle or a small bubble to be examined and classified, but the system as a whole stood there fairly secured, and theoretical physics approached visibly that degree of perfection which, for example, geometry has had already for centuries.'	Albert Einstein, 1917 'No matter how we may single out a complex from nature ... its theoretical treatment will never prove to be ultimately conclusive ... I believe that this process of deepening of theory has no limits.'
Heinrich Hertz, 1875 'Sometimes I really regret that I did not live in those times when there was still so much that was new; to be sure enough much is yet unknown, but I do not think that it will be possible to discover anything easily nowadays that would lead us to revise our entire outlook as radically as was possible in the days when telescopes and microscopes were still new.'	Lewis Thomas, 1963 (approx.) 'On any Tuesday morning, if asked, a good working scientist will tell you with some self-satisfaction that the affairs of his field are nicely in order, that things are finally looking clear and making sense, and all is well. But come back again on another Tuesday, and the roof may have just fallen in on his life's work.'
Lord Kelvin, 1900 'There is nothing new to be discovered in physics now. All that remains is more and more precise measurement.'	John Maddox, 1998 'Quite apart from the demand for more applications of science, there is also not yet an end in sight to the process of

	inquiry. The problems that remain unsolved are gargantuan. They will occupy our children and their children and on and on for perhaps even the rest of time.'
Albert Michelson, 1894 'The more important fundamental laws and facts of physical science have all been discovered, and these are now so firmly established that the possibility of their ever being supplanted in consequence of new discoveries is exceedingly remote ... Our future discoveries must be looked for in the sixth place of decimals.'	

However, there is an opposing view, also shown in Box 2.3 – that having major principles in place to direct their work frees scientists to make discoveries that will further improve society and our standard of living. Consequently, science has never been more alive as a field than it is today. John Maddox, a former editor of the science journal *Nature*, promotes this view in his book *What Remains to be Discovered* (1998). In Chapter 5 we discuss genius scientists (see page 106) working in key fields, who may yet make truly major discoveries that add to our list of fundamental principles. Questions such as these are all subject to current research:

♦ what is consciousness?
♦ can the laws of physics be unified?
♦ how do cells differentiate to make all the body organs?
♦ what is the Universe made of?
♦ why do humans have so few genes?
♦ how far can we take nanotechnology?
♦ what can replace fossil fuels, and when?

Science is not dead – but it will live differently in the future.

Finally, we consider possible dead-ends – questions that science can't answer. These include:

♦ why did the Big Bang happen?
♦ what happened before the Big Bang?

♦ is there another Universe?
♦ how many chemical elements are there?
♦ how did evolution start?
♦ should people be able to choose the sex of their babies?
♦ should science be used for developing weapons?

Scientists work within the framework of twenty-first-century science, and finding answers to these is beyond the limit of possibility at the moment. Will science be able to answer these questions? Or must we be satisfied with the fundamental theories we have now? Whether or not we agree with Horgan, with active scientists in our midst, the future will continue to be full of change and development.

2.4 Summary

Scientific developments:

♦ can occur in jumps – as scientists think of new theories to test, from evidence already collected
♦ have contributed enormously to our wellbeing and quality of life
♦ are occurring all the time – but we may question if this will continue.

There are questions that science cannot answer. These may be ethical questions for society, or questions that go beyond the realms of scientific discovery.
In the following two chapters, we start to unpick how science works more precisely, examining the roles theories, evidence and experiments play in making discoveries.

References and resources

Brekke, A. and Egeland, A. (1994) *Nordlyset*. Oslo, Norway: Grøndahl and Dreyer Forlag.

Egeland, A., Henriksen, E.K. and Henriksen, T. (1997) *Nordlys*. Temahefte 3. Oslo: Fysisk Institutt.

Griffiths, C. and Brock, A. (2003) Twentieth century mortality trends in England and Wales. *Health Statistics Quarterly* 18: 5–17.

Horgan, J. (1996) *The End of Science*. New York: Broadway Books.

Jago, L. (2001) *The Northern Lights*. London: Hamish Hamilton.

Maddox, J. (1998) *What Remains to Be Discovered*. London: Macmillan.

Marks, J. (1983) *Science and the Making of the Modern World*. Oxford: Heinemann.

Northern lights

For northern lights photographs and information about Kristian Birkeland (the site is in Norwegian, but the pictures of Birkeland's work are superior to any other): www.teknisk museum.no/no/forskning/birkeland/birkeland.htm

Folklore: legends and myths of the aurora: http://webexhibits. org/causesofcolor/4C.html

Antarctic Connection: aurora australis – southern lights: www.antarcticconnection.com/antarctic/weather/aurora.shtml

History of medicine

Statistics on every aspect of life in the UK are available from the Government website www.statistics.gov.uk – for specific issues, click on UK Snapshot and select Health. The data used in the activities here are available at: www.statistics.gov.uk/articles/HSQ/ MortalityTrends_HSQ18.pdf

Information about primitive health beliefs, myths and old wives tales can be found at: www.answers.com/topic/traditional-health-beliefs-practices? cat=health www.freeessays.cc/db/4/alx83.shtml

Old wives' tales can be found at: www.kidshealth.org/parent/ general/aches/old_wives_tales.html

The life of William Beaumont is described well at: www.james. com/beaumont/dr_life.htm

Pictures of prints in the Royal Collection are available from www.royalcollection.org.uk

The USA's National Institute of Health includes Islamic and western European medieval manuscripts, films and videos and anatomy books, such as the work of Vesalius: www.nlm.nih.gov/hmd

The Karolinska Institute in Sweden features sections on Mesopotamian, traditional Chinese, traditional Indian, classical Islamic and western medicine, as well as a thorough section on the history of diseases: www.mic.ki.se/History.html

The schools history website is specifically designed for students' use and is organised along similar themes: www.schools history.org.uk/medicine.htm

The end of science?

Discussion of the controversy raised by John Horgan's book, *The End of Science*, can be read at: www.edge.org/documents/archive/edge16.html

Theories

3.1 Why do you need this chapter?

The aims of this chapter are to:

♦ help ensure the terms theory, hypothesis and law are understood and used correctly
♦ describe what children understand by scientific theory
♦ explore whether scientific theories must always be tentative.

Achieving the first aim is important because these terms are often used interchangeably – is it correct to do this, or should we be more careful? Can distinct meanings be justified? If we incorrectly use all three terms to mean the same thing, this may cause misunderstandings. We need to teach these terms accurately, and ensure they are used correctly.

In science, theories are given great importance – in school science, most of the theories we teach are well established. Helping students understand what a scientific theory is will help them appreciate the process of doing science. We review the understandings children have of 'theory', and suggest ways of addressing these.

The third aim attempts to address how scientific theories change status from being questions subject to testing, to facts accepted as true.

To understand these points is to get to the heart of understanding science. Scientists use methods in their work that we regard as systematic, organised, thorough and reliable. Theories are produced, tested by experiment, then accepted, rejected or tested again. This process of refinement leads to the development of scientific knowledge. This system, based on Karl Popper's philosophy of science (Chapter 1, page 16) is widely accepted as illustrating how science works, and is implicit in what many of us think of as 'doing science'. Understanding what is meant by a scientific theory is therefore central to understanding science.

We found in writing this chapter that a great deal of confusion exists – for example, a simple internet search does not produce clear definitions. Try typing 'definition of scientific theory' into a search engine. Defining a theory is something that sounds simple, but in reality is difficult. We hope that this chapter helps to clarify your thinking, as writing it did ours.

The activities have been designed to help clarify students' thinking. We deliberately use information that is not normally seen in school science lessons, as we wanted to go beyond the usual and avoid telling partial truths that can be frustrating for both students and teachers. Students really do appreciate the truth, even if it is something they cannot fully understand.

3.2 Activities

◆ *The development of atomic theory*

Time required: about 40 minutes
NC link: PoS 1a, b; 4c

Learning outcomes

◆ To understand that:
  – scientific theories develop in jumps
  – scientists develop new theories based on weaknesses in existing ones.
◆ To realise that theories are products of human creativity.

Background

The notion of atoms was first proposed by the Greek philosophers Democritus and Leucippus in about 2000BC. The word atom comes from the Greek *atomos*, meaning 'uncuttable'. As atoms are too small to be seen directly, scientists have developed models representing what they think atoms might be like, based on experimental observations. These are approximations based on interpretation of experimental evidence. We use the word 'model' as a way of saying 'theory of atomic structure'. Analogies might include toy dolls (a doll is a model of a baby or person), toy cars, model aeroplanes, or images in computer games. Each model bears some resemblance to reality, but is not the complete picture.

The table 'Atomic theory: models describing atomic structure' (versions A and B), provided on the CD, shows theories (models) of atomic structure that have been proposed over the past 200 years, together with the names of scientists and brief supporting and contradictory evidence. Version A ends with

Rutherford's planetary motion model, while version B includes higher-level material.

The table shows how each model supersedes the previous one by meeting the contradictory evidence for earlier versions. Like toy dolls, no model is perfect or complete. All the models have explanatory power – they can be used to explain one or more aspects of the behaviour of atoms. All the models are creative products – they have been thought up by scientists. They all have an element of truth and value about them: for example, we use the billiard ball model when teaching kinetic particle theory. Others would have too much detail. The Bohr model is useful (and the billiard ball model nonsensical) when teaching the arrangement of electrons in atoms, because it provides an explanation for simple emission spectra. The final one, based on Schrödinger's wave equation, is the best model for describing the behaviour of electrons in atoms.

Work continues to establish more precisely the components of subatomic particles, the forces that prevent atoms from collapse and those that hold nuclei together.

Two versions of the data table are available to permit differentiation. However, students should be introduced to higher-level aspects of atomic theory so they see a complete picture of the events. The point is for students to realise that scientists have gone far beyond the standard view of the atom that is presented in school science lessons – they need to know that there is more to atomic structure than protons, electrons and neutrons.

Starter activity

Prompt discussion about what children think a theory is, using one of the scenarios – Rusting, Balloons or Germs (adapted from Driver *et al.*, 1996) (Theories task sheet provided on the CD). Responses could be grouped using these headings:

♦ fact
♦ explanation
♦ testable by experiment
♦ helps you understand something.

These tie in with the information presented in section 3.3. Ask students to back up their answers: 'why do you think that?'; 'do you have another example?' could be good follow-up questions.

Main activity

Requirements: data tables and question sheets (provided on the CD).

Discuss the data tables, drawing out key changes as suggested below.

Versions A and B

♦ Solid atom (billiard ball).
♦ Non-solid atom (Rutherford).

Version B only

♦ Electrons in orbits (Bohr).
♦ More complicated orbits (Sommerfeld).
♦ Electrons in 3D orbits with different shapes (Shrödinger; pronounced 'Shruhdinger').

Questions are provided corresponding to each version of the table. If all students use the same data source, explanation may be required of terms such as gold foil experiment, quantum mechanics and emission spectra.

A difficult idea to grasp is that in the Rutherford and subsequent models, most of the atom is empty space.

The task would work well with an opportunity to research further information using ICT facilities. Students could develop their responses to questions by adding additional material, such as pictures of scientists and further information about the experiments.

Extending the task

Invite students to discuss or present their atomic theories, depending on the range and quality of their ideas. This should confirm the notion that theories are creative products of human invention.

Answers

Version A

1. a) answers will vary; b) people thought them up, based on evidence.
    c) 1805; d) 1925; e) 120; f) answers will vary; g) the new models explained evidence that the last one could not.
    h,i) Answers will vary; j) billiard ball – solid, no subatomic particles; Rutherford – mainly space, electrons orbiting a nucleus.
2. Answers will vary.

Version B

1. a) 1805; b) 1925; c) none was satisfactory as some evidence was always unexplained.
   d) Solid ball of matter; e) nucleus with particles, surrounded by electrons in different-shaped orbits.
   f) Shrödinger's, because it is closer to what evidence suggests an atom is like.
2. Dates from the data table.
   a) Rutherford – some may argue J.J. Thomson, but his model didn't predict space.
   b) The gold foil experiment showed the atom has a dense nucleus.
   c) Bohr's model.
   d) Newtonian mechanics predicted that atoms would collapse as electrons would eventually spiral into the nucleus.
3. It means they know the current theory is not perfect and further development is possible.
4. We still have not explained completely how positive charges can stay together in the nucleus when they should repel; also we don't know exactly what the particles are made of.
5. Answers will vary.

Plenary discussion

Reiterate that:

- each atomic structure theory is a model, invented by a scientist, based on evidence
- the models become more sophisticated
- a new model accounts for the contradictory evidence of older ones
- each theory has its uses, and none is perfect
- atomic theory can develop further – we can all have ideas.

Finally, ask students to review their ideas about what a theory is, returning to their starting views.

◆ *How true is a theory?*

Time required: about 30 minutes.
NC link: PoS 1c

Learning outcomes

- To understand that scientific theories:
  - are not always 'true'
  - have different degrees of truth.

♦ To understand that scientists do not always know for certain if a theory is true or not.

♦ To understand that collecting evidence helps scientists decide if a theory is true or false.

Background

Students often think that theories are simply pieces of knowledge that explain an event. In this activity, students are introduced to the possibility that theories can be correct, inconclusive or wrong. Three different theories are posed: 'the Earth is flat, not round'; 'mobile phones and masts cause cancer'; and 'human beings evolved from the apes'. Each is an example of a theory with different status – wrong, inconclusive, and widely accepted as correct, respectively. Through responding to questions, students are encouraged to realise the different degrees of 'truth' associated with scientific theories.

Starter activity

Play a version of the old-fashioned panel game 'Call my Bluff', in which opposing teams try to decide the true meaning of an obscure word from three alternatives. Some students will be better deceivers (in the nicest sense) than others. Give each of three students a different card with the definition of an obscure word on it. The card should indicate if the definition is true or false, but this secret must be kept by the student. Only one definition is true, the others are false. Each student reads his or her card in turn, perhaps with a sentence including the word, as if it were true, trying to be as convincing as possible. The rest of the class have to vote on whether they think each definition is true or false. After the vote, students reveal which definition was correct.

This can be repeated with as many words as you like – but two or three will suffice to make the point that it can be quite difficult to tell if someone is telling the truth or not. We may also have very fixed ideas about who is telling the truth. The same can happen in science – theories can be true or false, or we can be uncertain.

We have suggested a few obscure English words from http://phrontistery.info (provided on the CD). The true definitions are from the website, the false ones we have made up. The trick is to find words the students will never have heard of, so that the success of the game depends entirely on readers being convincing.

Main activity

Requirements: Task sheet (provided on the CD).

Option 1: Everyone looks at all three theories
All three theories can be presented to all students in the class, who work in groups on the answers to the questions.

Option 2: The class is divided into groups, each looking at one theory
In this case, students need to present their answers to the rest of the class, perhaps by preparing a poster or a PowerPoint presentation.

Answers to the questions

The Earth is flat

1. They refuse to believe scientific evidence, preferring the Bible's view.
2. No. Scientific evidence says the Earth is round.
3. We can't feel ourselves moving through space.
4. Views of Earth from space; the way the time of day changes around the globe; seasons show we are moving around the Sun; movements of the planets and stars around the Earth.

Mobile telephones and telephone masts cause cancer

1. People living near some masts and power lines have developed health problems, such as more cancer than in populations not living close to masts or power lines.
2. The evidence is not clear, and there could be other reasons for this.
3. For example, the amount and type of radiation given out does not cause cancer; lifestyles are responsible for many cancers, and maybe busy people tend to live in areas where there are masts; people in one area may be closely related so there may be a genetic link to the cancers.
4. Taking evidence over a long period and studying the populations who live near masts and power lines closely; carrying out experiments on animals (!) to see how they are affected by radiation.

Human beings evolved from apes

1. People could not believe they were not created directly by God; people were very resistant to changing views that were based on interpreting the Bible.

2. There is now much more scientific evidence to support the theory, e.g. from genetics, and people are less religious than they were in Victorian times. No evidence has been found that makes the theory false.
3. Look at how genetic traits are carried from one generation to another; fossil records; study of how close our genes are to chimpanzees.
4. Answers will vary – the basic theory is not likely to change, but more information about detailed mechanisms may mean some changes to our understanding about how evolution occurs.

Plenary discussion

Draw out the following points.

♦ All these are scientific theories.
♦ The theories are true to different extents – what is the order from least to most true?
♦ Scientists can prove a theory right or wrong – but people don't always accept this.
♦ Scientists don't always know if a theory is right or wrong.
♦ Scientists have to keep on collecting evidence to prove or disprove theories.

Compare with 'Call my Bluff' – it can be difficult to tell what is true, and we need to be sceptical. What could we do to check if the definitions were true or false?

♦ *Theories and evidence*

Time required: about 20 minutes, longer if the activity is extended
NC link: PoS 1c

Learning outcomes

♦ To understand that theories explain observations.
♦ To understand that theories can be supported or rejected on the basis of evidence.

Background

This simple card sort activity (provided on CD) centres on the principle that theories have explanatory power. Students have to match theory statements with evidence in favour, and against. To make this more difficult, either the 'Evidence in favour', or the 'Evidence against cards' could be removed, so students have to think this up for themselves.

Evidence in favour	Theory	Evidence against
Southern England had a drought last summer	Patterns of rainfall are changing due to human activity on Earth	Southern England suffering heavy rain and flooding the following summer
Pure water boils at 100 °C	A change of state from liquid to gas occurs due to increased kinetic energy of the particles. For water this occurs at 100 °C	Finding a sample of water that does not boil at 100 °C
Green plants release oxygen into the atmosphere	All green plants can photosynthesise: this reaction produces their own food. Oxygen is a product of photosynthesis	Finding a green plant that does not release oxygen into the atmosphere
Tides follow the pattern of the Moon's movement around the Earth	The Earth exerts a gravitational pull on objects nearby, such as the Moon	Finding a tide pattern that does not match the movement of the Moon
The weather in the northern hemisphere is warmer in the summer than in the winter	The Earth orbits around the Sun. The tilt of the Earth is responsible for our seasons	Experiencing a winter season in the northern hemisphere that is warmer than the summer
A car is not a living organism. A plant is a living organism	All living things respire, reproduce, move, excrete, grow, are sensitive, and need nutrition	Finding a car that meets all the criteria for a living organism
Chemical reactions always produce new substances, with nothing left over	The same amount of 'stuff' always exists in the Universe. Matter cannot be created or destroyed	Seeing a chemical reaction in which matter is either created or destroyed
Volcanoes occur at the edges of tectonic plates	The Earth's crust is a mobile set of plates floating on a molten core. Volcanoes are one feature produced where these meet	Discovering a volcano that is not at the edge of two tectonic plates
The closest relative of the human being is the chimpanzee	We evolved by natural selection from the great apes over a long period of time	Finding evidence that human beings evolved separately from the chimpanzee, e.g. human remains that are older than any chimpanzee remains

Plenary discussion

The discussion should draw out the following points.

♦ Whether it was easy or difficult to think up the evidence for and against specific theories – which ones were hardest? Note that these could be the ones we are most used to accepting as true.

♦ Theories seek to explain observations of natural phenomena.

♦ Some theories are more certain or true than others – the chance of finding a car that could be described as alive for example, is very small. Evidence contradicting some of the other theories is perhaps more likely.

- Reliability of evidence – some of the statements refer to one event – is this enough? When is scientific evidence sufficient to be regarded as reliable?
- Why are some theories still argued over, while others are accepted as true facts?
- What happens when contradictory evidence is produced? – Scientists modify their theories or reject them; how easy is this in practice?

3.3 Background information

◆ *What are the differences between theory, hypothesis and law?*

In this section we discuss definitions of these three words, and where their meanings overlap. The aim here is to clarify understanding and suggest when each term should be used to minimise confusion.

In colloquial use, theory most often means 'uncertain'. In everyday language we may say, 'Yes, in theory, that's OK' meaning that on balance, what is being referred to may happen or can be agreed to. 'In theory' acts as a get-out clause should a situation turn out differently from how we expect. Theory in this context means something vague or imprecise, or relates to an event that may or may not happen. In science, a theory can mean something that is certain, or that is still subject to testing. This, coupled with the colloquial meaning, causes confusion. A good dictionary gives a range of definitions for the word theory. Here are seven from ours (Onions, 1986, Volume II, p. 2281):

1. mental view or contemplation
2. a conception or mental scheme of something to be done, or the method of doing it
3. a hypothesis proposed as speculation or conjecture
4. a hypothesis that has been confirmed or established by experiment and is accepted as accounting for the known facts
5. a systematic statement of rules or principles to be followed
6. a scheme or system of ideas or statements held as an explanation for a group of facts or phenomena
7. a statement of general laws, principles or causes for something known or observed.

Reasons for problems with the word theory become obvious – the word has a range of meanings, showing different levels of certainty. The first three listed above indicate that theories are uncertain and not proved, while the latter four imply that a theory is something that is proven, and has explanatory power. Two of the definitions have 'hypothesis' embedded in them, and one includes 'laws'.

The first three definitions show that a theory can be an idea that comes into our head – at the highest level of science, thought experiments such as Einstein's riding on a beam of light, or Kekulé's imagining of the benzene ring structure, are examples. Scientists have to start somewhere with ideas about what might cause a phenomenon: the account of the northern lights in Chapter 2 is a good example. A theory need not be immediately subject to experimental testing, nor need it be true, or proven. These meanings allow scientists to speculate and propose ideas, each time using the word 'theory' in their work.

Experimental testing of theories and collecting evidence to support or refute them are found in definition 4. A theory becomes established as true when tests provide supporting evidence. A theory can be rejected or refined if experimental evidence does not support it.

Definitions 4–7 state that theories can have certainty and are not always tentative. Certainty is implied in definition 5, and clearly stated in definitions 4, 6 and 7. These definitions also show that a theory can cover a broad range of points in one statement. Definition 5 gives us the meaning: 'according to theory X, Y should happen' – a theory can have predictive power. Definitions 6 and 7 mean that we can say with justification that some theories are, to all intents and purposes, accepted as explanations. The implication here is that we can claim some theories as true or, if that is too strong, very unlikely to change.

The point is that 'theory' does have a variety of meanings, and students need to see that this is the case. A theory can be speculative, explanatory, and/or true. A speculative theory could be true – but we don't yet know because it hasn't been tested. A theory regarded as true will have supporting evidence backing this up. Any theory, whether proven or not, can have explanatory power and cover a wide range of situations.

The overlap between theory, hypothesis and law needs clarification. Interestingly, the dictionary defines a scientific hypothesis (in a rather long-winded phrase) as something much less certain than a theory (Onions, 1986, Volume I, p. 1010):

'A provisional supposition which accounts for known facts and serves as a starting point for further investigation by which it may be proved or disproved'.

This definition fits with number 4 in the list for theory, above. Use of both theory and hypothesis in setting up investigations appears to be justified from these two definitions. However, we suggest that hypothesis should be reserved for these situations only. When we look at more general meanings for the word, we find much more uncertainty:

'Something assumed to be true without proof'

'A mere assumption or guess'

If the term hypothesis is used any more widely than in the sense of a proposition for an experiment, this could cause confusion. We recommend that hypothesis is used when setting up investigations and uncertainty is certain – hopefully that's clear!

Finally, the dictionary offers this, again long-winded, definition of law, in the scientific sense:

'In the sciences of observation, a theoretical principle deduced from particular facts, expressible by the statement that a particular phenomenon always occurs if certain conditions be present' (Onions, Volume I, p. 1185).

This definition hangs on 'theoretical principle', 'particular phenomenon' and 'always occurs'. A law does not explain a phenomenon by itself. A law is a statement that can be used to support a theory that does attempt an explanation. This fits with definition 7 in the above list. A law is specific, applying under certain conditions. As scientists, we can all think of laws in our own fields that meet these criteria. Laws provide the back-up for theories, permitting calculations and providing supporting statements. They are not the theories themselves. Box 3.1 illustrates this using Newton's law of gravity as an example.

Box 3.1 The law of gravity – part of Newton's theory about planets and objects

In 1687, Isaac Newton's most famous work, *Principia Mathematica*, was published. It included a law of gravity (more accurately called the law of universal gravitation). Newton expressed this mathematically so that physicists could describe what happens to falling objects. He set this within a wider theory about planets and other objects in the Universe, claiming that all objects have masses that exert forces on each other. When objects make direct contact, forces are exchanged. When objects are apart, forces exert a pull between them.

Newton's theory was an attempt to explain his observations of the behaviour of objects in the world around him. Working from this, he defined a more specific range of principles and relationships. For example, big masses exert bigger forces – that is, the size of the force is proportional to the mass. In the case of the law of gravity, gravity is suggested as a name for the force exerted by a big mass (the Earth) on objects close by. We call this a law because it is the principle supporting the theory about planets and other objects. The law is part of the theory, not the theory itself. We often refer to laws independently of theories, giving a false impression as to their status.

We need to remember the bigger picture – the law is part of this. To complete our example, we can refer to the law of gravity if we want to explain its fundamental role in our understanding of why objects always fall back to Earth. To obtain a full picture of the status of the law, we should also discuss its context within Newton's theory.

Problems occur between theory and law because, when teaching, we often separate laws from the theories they support. Textbooks use the terms interchangeably; we see 'law of gravity' and 'theory of gravity' for the same item. Laws are not seen in context, but are taught as isolated items of scientific knowledge. Also, we do not always clarify that laws apply only under certain conditions. That a law does not apply when physical conditions change comes as a surprise to post-16 science students.

So, to summarise:

♦ theory – a tentative or proven explanation for a phenomenon
♦ hypothesis – a proposal for an experiment where the outcome is uncertain
♦ law – a statement that supports a theory and applies only under certain conditions.

♦ *Children's ideas about scientific theories*

Having analysed dictionary definitions and hopefully clarified our own thinking about theory, hypothesis and law, we can now look at children's understandings. These were investigated in a major UK-based project in the mid-1990s (Driver *et al.*, 1996) that sought children's ideas about the nature of science. We report the findings relating to work on children's ideas about scientific theories.

A theory is ...

Students grasp the concept of theory in a limited but varied way. Aspects of the range of colloquial and scientific uses for the term theory and, perhaps, a lack of explicit teaching are found. Children have four main suggestions about what a theory is:

♦ a vague idea, or knowing something about a situation
♦ a prediction
♦ an explanation for a specific event
♦ a general explanation that applies in a range of settings.

One-third of 9–12-year-olds thought a theory was a vague idea, but only a few older children said this. Few students, of all ages, thought of theory as a prediction. Thinking of a theory as a general explanation that applies in more than one situation was present to a greater extent among older children, with around three-quarters of 16-year-olds giving this suggestion, compared with fewer than a quarter of 9-year-olds (*op. cit.*, pp. 93–4). These are rather vague suggestions, suggesting that children's meanings for theory are not well formed.

A theory is just knowledge that describes a phenomenon

Some children regard a theory as a piece of knowledge that can be taken for granted. In other words, a theory is a statement that tells us what the world is like; children are willing to accept such statements at face value and hence regard theories as true facts. An example (*op. cit.*, p. 94) relates to milk going sour more rapidly when left out of the fridge. A 16-year-old commented that this occurs because 'When you put [milk] in the fridge it doesn't get rid of [the microbes]. It (*sic*) just ... they don't grow as quickly.' The student offers a theory that provides a straightforward explanation, but does not connect theory to evidence, in effect saying 'It just is like that'.

A theory relates to a real-world phenomenon that is testable

More sophisticated is the understanding that theory is something that can be tested by experiment, to obtain proof of correctness. This comes from children's experiences of scientific method, when theory means 'testable hypothesis', its truth being determined by experiments involving controlling variables. More complex reasoning involves links being made between variables. For example, the theory 'microbes in milk grow better in warm temperatures than cold' was tested by two 16-year-olds, who said in interview:

'Student 1: We've already done experiments ... We had some milk left out and some milk put in the fridge and dipped our fingers in them and took down the results ... It went off quicker in the heat.

Student 2: We put [the milk] in the freezer ... and [the microbes] don't do anything [because] it's too cold for them.' (*op. cit.*, pp. 94–5)

The students do not question that the basic statement might not be true. They seek only to confirm it as true by experiment. Different variables may contribute, such as the temperature, any prior treatment of the milk (raw, pasteurised or sterilised), and the form of storage (sealed plastic container, glass bottle with foil cap, open jug, carton, etc.). The students have to decide which variables to test to support the theory, not whether formally to challenge its truth. Older children are willing to accept that absolute proof is not obtainable, saying 'you can never be absolutely sure'.

A theory as a model

A few 16-year-olds show a much more sophisticated way of thinking, understanding theory as a model. They relate the properties of the model to observed changes in the system it represents. This raises the possibility that the model may need changing, and hence that a theory is a conjecture with provisional status. This is closest to the notional 'agreed' scientific definition mentioned above (page 70). To illustrate this, two students discussed a task involving a balloon fitted over the narrow neck of a metal tin. The balloon fills with air when the base of the tin is heated, regardless of whether the tin is upright or upside-down.

'Student 1: *The air molecules* are still being heated and *have got all the energy* and *are moving about just as much as they were before when it was the right way up*.

Student 2: ... *hot air does rise* ... it's just that other things happen as well so ... The hot air would still be going to the top of the tin and then cooling and pouring down, back down, again because of the ...

Student 1: [Yes]. But it also happens *that the particles jiggle around and expand*. So (it still fills).

Student 2: [Yes]' (*op. cit.*, pp. 95–6, italics added)

Both students propose theoretical models using the behaviour of air molecules: these 'have energy' and 'jiggle and expand'. Although neither is wholly right, the discussion indicates that the students accept the conjectural nature of their models, and that both are open to question.

A theory is not ...

Children do not think of a theory as something imagined or created by a person or scientist. The strongest tendency is to link a theory to an observable phenomenon and to connect this to experimental testing.

Children do not easily understand the limitations of theories. They think that theories can be linked to phenomena in unproblematic ways, so regard them as facts that can be accepted. Only a few older students are sceptical about absolute proof and consider theories as conjectures.

What might we expect students to know and understand about theories?

The research findings presented here indicate that secondary-age students think that a theory:

♦ can be tested by experiment, usually involving controlling variables
♦ is a fact about a natural phenomenon
♦ helps them understand how the world works
♦ provides a general explanation for events.

In terms of how science works, this view is limited. We suggest that students should also understand that a theory can be:

♦ the product of someone's creative, imaginative thinking
♦ subject to change over time
♦ competing with another theory
♦ purely speculative.

3.4 Summary

Theories, hypotheses and laws have different meanings. We repeat here our definitions as:

♦ theory – a tentative or proven explanation for a phenomenon
♦ hypothesis – a proposal for an experiment where the outcome is uncertain
♦ law – a statement that supports a theory and applies only under certain conditions.

Children have mixed ideas about what constitutes a scientific theory. We recommend that teachers take time to find out what their students think, and take this into account in planning lessons that teach explicitly what a scientific theory is.

3.5 References and resources

Driver, R., Leach, J., Millar, R. and Scott, P. (1996) *Young People's Images of Science*. Buckingham: Open University Press.

Onions, C.T. (ed.) (1986) *The Shorter English Dictionary*. London: Guild Publishing.

White, M. (1997) *Isaac Newton, The Last Sorcerer*. London: Fourth Estate.

Obscure English words can be obtained from http://phrontistery.info

Atomic theory development

A website giving brief information about a number of scientists who contributed to our understanding of atomic structure, with clear photos and good diagrams: http://library.thinkquest.org/C006669/data/Chem/atomic/development.html

Bill Bryson's highly readable *A Short History of Nearly Everything* (2003, London: Black Swan Books) includes a good range of references to atomic structure.

Tony Hey and Patrick Walters' *The Quantum Universe* (1989, Cambridge: Cambridge University Press) provides an excellent account of basic quantum physics. The book includes some excellent photos that help students understand the small size of atoms.

The flat Earth theory

There is an organisation called the Flat Earth Society that has a website. This is almost certainly a spoof, but even (or especially) is worth a look: www.alaska.net/~clund/e_djublonskopf/Flatearthsociety.htm

Other American websites discuss the flat Earth theory and its origins, for example: http://home1.gte.net/deleyd/religion/galileo/flatearth.html www.talkorigins.org/faqs/flatearth.html

Definitive information about the flat Earth theory can be found in Christine Garwood's book *Flat Earth: The History of an Infamous Idea* (2007, London: Macmillan).

Mobile telephones and telephone masts cause cancer

This topic is currently hotly debated. Reports from both sides are available, for example:

Promoting a link
www.telegraph.co.uk/news/main.jhtml?xml=/news/2007/08/30/
    nmobile130.xml
www.cancer-health.org

Against the link
www.spiked-online.com/index.php?/site/article/3819
www.timesonline.co.uk/tol/news/uk/health/article2442009.ece

Informative
Government research report: www.parliament.uk/commons/
    lib/research/rp2001/rp01-111.pdf
The original Stewart Report from 2000:
    www.iegmp.org.uk/report/text.htm

Human beings evolved from apes

Charles Darwin's original text was entitled *On the Origin of
    Species by Means of Natural Selection, or the Preservation of
    Favoured Races in the Struggle for Life*, and published in 1859.
    It can be read on the web at
    www.talkorigins.org/faqs/origin.html
There are many websites, mainly American, that discuss
    evolution, but this is mainly as a theory that challenges
    creation – there is little balance.

4 Experiments and evidence

4.1 Why do you need this chapter?

The aims of this chapter are to:

♦ show that doing experiments and/or collecting evidence are central activities in scientists' work
♦ illustrate that evidence can support or refute a theory or hypothesis
♦ describe children's ideas about scientific experiments and questions.

The first two aims are quite basic – some scientists describe themselves as 'theoretical', meaning that they don't do experiments, but most would agree that carrying out experiments in a laboratory and/or collecting evidence in another setting constitutes a significant part of their work. As we noted in Chapter 3, scientists can propose theories and test them by experiments and/or by collecting evidence. On the basis of their findings, theories can be accepted, modified or rejected. Experiments and evidence are crucial to building scientific knowledge. Theories provide the 'wrapping' or framework, and may have different levels of certainty. The Background information (page 83) connects theories, experiments and evidence with Karl Popper's philosophy of science (see Chapter 1).

In this chapter, we use 'hypothesis' and 'theory' interchangeably because we are discussing the collection of experimental data. As explained in Chapter 3, under these circumstances using both terms as synonyms is acceptable according to the definitions of these words. We suggest that clearly explaining this point to students may help them realise that 'theory' has different meanings in different circumstances.

The third aim is met by reviewing research on children's ideas in this area (page 85). We find this helpful in setting the scene for the kinds of problems children have with what seem to be quite simple aspects of doing science. We strongly encourage reading this section when preparing to teach any of the activities. We have used unusual sources of information for these, in the hope that students will be stimulated by their novelty.

4.2 Activities

Three activities are suggested, each lasting about 40 minutes:

♦ a hypothesis that was proved wrong – how the Earth's features were formed
♦ a hypothesis that was proved correct – the real cause of stomach ulcers
♦ a hypothesis that is inconclusive – the case of the Martian stone.

♦ *A hypothesis that was proved wrong – how the Earth's features were formed*

Time required: about 40 minutes
NC link: 1c, 3a, 3c, 4c

Learning outcomes

♦ To understand that:
  – science involves thinking up testable hypotheses
  – 'testable' means 'can be proved true or false'.
♦ To realise that scientists will reject a hypothesis where evidence shows that the idea it expresses is incorrect.

Background

The two theories summarised in the speech bubbles (see task sheet on the CD) are based on real theories circulating in the nineteenth century. The scientists' names are also real: Louis Agassiz (1807–73) was a Swiss scientist and Charles Lyell (1797–1875) was British. Each supported a different theory explaining how the Earth's features formed.

The catastrophe theory proposed that the Earth's features were formed in a series of major events, including the Biblical flood. Each catastrophe destroyed all life and resulted in the Earth's surface reforming. Afterwards, new life formed spontaneously.

The uniformitarian theory proposed that glaciers larger than those seen today (and larger than those seen in the nineteenth century) covered large parts of northern Europe. The glaciers eroded the fjords and the English Lake District, and contributed to other features such as Arthur's Seat in Edinburgh.

Agassiz initially thought that the Biblical flood caused the Earth's features. He changed his mind when he went to the Alps in 1836 with another scientist, Frenchman Jean de

Charpentier. The following year, in 1837, Agassiz proposed the daring hypothesis that glaciers and ice sheets covered much more of the northern hemisphere, from the North Pole to the Mediterranean and Caspian Seas. He developed this into support for the catastrophe theory, inventing the concept of a global 'Ice Age' that was the last great catastrophe to blight the Earth, resulting in the extinction of all living things.

Charles Lyell proposed the uniformitarian theory. This argued that changes to the Earth's surface were more gradual, and that other features such as volcanic eruptions could have contributed as well. This theory noted that changes were still going on.

Resolution of the argument occurred gradually as evidence from different sources was collected.

♦ The theory of evolution by natural selection indicated that organisms developed gradually, suggesting that extinction followed by spontaneous generation was extremely unlikely to have resulted in the diversity of species seen on Earth.
♦ Changes in the Earth's orbit were believed to have occurred, causing changes in seasonal temperatures and hence more than one ice age, over a very long period.

Agassiz's theory that there was one global ice age that resulted in the extinction of all species was proved false. Nevertheless, questions remain: the cause(s) of extinction of the dinosaurs and creatures such as the mammoth; the survival mechanisms of certain organisms under severely cold conditions and precisely how the Earth's temperatures have changed. Agassiz was partly right, in that Greenland was found to be covered with ice, and major ice sheets coated large areas of North America. Agassiz's work demonstrates how scientists make clear statements based on instinct, without supporting evidence. When evidence supports a bold idea, the scientist responsible is often regarded as a 'genius'. Agassiz was a talented scientist who had the courage to make a falsifiable hypothesis. That it was proved wrong is just in the nature of the scientific game.

Charles Lyell is regarded as a highly influential geologist. His book *Principles of Geology*, first printed in the 1830s, put geology on a modern footing with other sciences. His work supported Charles Darwin's and Alfred Russel Wallace's theories of evolution by natural selection, which relied on there being time for species to evolve.

Teaching points

♦ The two theories have complicated names – this was typical for nineteenth-century Victorian science.
♦ The theories are contradictory – the Earth cannot have been formed by catastrophes and by gradual processes at the same time. So one must be right and the other wrong.
♦ Quality of evidence is important in deciding whether a theory should be rejected or accepted. Further evidence can also be sought.
♦ Theories may take a long time to be accepted or rejected. This can extend beyond the lifetime of the scientist.

Plenary discussion

♦ Ask students to sort the evidence cards (provided on the CD) and say which theory they ended up supporting, and what their reasons were.
♦ Indicate that, over time, one theory was proved to be correct and the other false.
♦ If some picked the catastrophe theory, discuss why scientists can be led down the wrong track – evidence can be convincing, and it can be difficult to reject ideas.
♦ Draw out the points that scientists can make proposals, but have to accept that they can be wrong as well as right.
♦ Theories may be partly right and wrong.
♦ Some evidence may still be unexplained – theories are not perfect.

Evidence for Louis's theory	**Evidence for Charles's theory**
The woolly mammoth was suddenly made extinct	U-shaped fjords (in Scandinavia) and U-shaped valleys were known to have been caused by ice
Greenland was once covered with ice	The Earth's orbit changed gradually, causing temperature changes at different points on the Earth's surface
The Arctic ice sheet is shrinking – this ice sheet must have been much bigger	Fossil records show that organisms evolve continuously
The dinosaurs became extinct	Other events, such as river flows changing and volcanic eruptions, can also cause the Earth's features
The Bible describes a massive flood that wiped out every living thing except Noah, his family and the creatures in the ark	The theory of evolution by natural selection explains that organisms developed gradually over long periods
'Ice ages' happened in many places over the Earth's surface	Changes in the Earth's surface are still seen today, such as sea eroding the coastline, volcanoes erupting, lakes changing shape

◆ *A hypothesis that was proved correct – the real cause of stomach ulcers*

Time required: about 40 minutes
NC link: 1c, 4a

Learning outcomes

◆ To understand that:
- scientists produce explanations for phenomena by doing experiments
- scientists can start with a hypothesis, do experiments then develop a theory.

◆ To find out about a contemporary scientific discovery.

Figure 4.1 *Barry J. Marshall and J. Robin Warren*

Background

Australian doctors Barry J. Marshall and J. Robin Warren won the Nobel Prize in Physiology or Medicine in 2005, for their theory that stomach ulcers are caused by a bacterial infection, not stress-related illness. Their work took over 20 years, beginning with a hypothesis, which was tested by experiments and collection of evidence. Eventually they had enough evidence to confirm their hypothesis. The story clearly illustrates the principles of Popper's scientific method (see Chapter 1). The activity takes students through the stages of this development.

Teaching points

The starter activity asks students to identify what they think is a scientific question.

The main activity is a directed activity related to text (DART) to help students understand:

- the starting point for the doctors' work
- how the hypothesis was tested
- the nature of the evidence collected
- how the hypothesis was confirmed and developed.

Use the fact sheet and questions provided on the CD.

To take this further, discuss the implications of the discovery for people suffering from intestinal ulcers, leading to an appreciation of why this won the Nobel Prize.

Starter activity

What is a 'scientific' question? Ask the class to read a series of questions and pick out the ones they think are scientific. They must also have a reason why they think it is scientific.

To extend this, ask:

- why are the others not scientific?
- what, in general, makes a question scientific?

Plenary discussion

Help students to see the difference between scientific and non-scientific questions. For example, a scientific question must be:

- testable by experiment
- linked with a theory/hypothesis.

Return to the notion of scientific questions. What made the doctors' hypothesis – about bacteria causing stomach ulcers – a good question to ask?

◆ *A hypothesis that is inconclusive – the case of the Martian stone*

Time required: about 40 minutes
NC link: 1b, d, 2d, 3a, c

Learning outcomes

- To understand that scientists can generate hypotheses from evidence.
- To consider alternative ways of interpreting data.
- To understand that scientists cannot always be certain about what is true.

Background

The classic scientific method is not the only way in which science accumulates knowledge. The case of the Martian stone is an example of how scientists collect evidence, interpret it, then generate a hypothesis. The hypothesis in itself makes a contribution to knowledge, and stimulates further activity.

In 1996, a team of scientists from NASA (the North American Space Agency) and Stanford University in California, USA announced their belief that bacteria lived on Mars about 4 billion years ago. They based their reasoning on their analysis of a meteorite found in Antarctica in 1984. The main activity gives excerpts from a news report about this discovery. The report indicates that scientists had:

♦ collected the stone sample
♦ carried out a range of different tests on the stone
♦ interpreted the data from the tests
♦ generated a hypothesis to explain the data.

This turns scientific method upside-down – scientists investigated an unknown rock sample, generating a hypothesis on the basis of their results. Their work stimulates controversy because no-one else has found evidence for life on Mars. The hypothesis may or may not be true: the scientists admit that other explanations are possible, even though they believe their interpretation.

The task also gives alternative evidence so students can suggest other interpretations.

Teaching points

Invite students to explain what the scientists did – they tested rock samples and found one that looked different. Use task sheet – part 1 provided on the CD. They carried out more tests, and found strange structures that they thought could be from tiny animals that had died billions of years ago. The age and nature of the rock suggested it could be from Mars. Their hypothesis is there must have been living organisms on Mars billions of years ago.

The evidence generated the hypothesis, not the other way round.

The hypothesis is being tested (see part 2 of the task sheet on the CD) and is not proven yet. Some information suggests that the rock and the structures in it are not from Mars, whereas other data cannot be explained as being from Earth.

Plenary discussion

Review the range of opinions in the class after discussion of part 2 of the task sheet on the CD.

Draw out the points that:

- scientists can come up with a bold idea (hypothesis) in the course of their everyday work
- ideas can come from evidence – we don't need the hypothesis first
- scientists are not always certain – evidence can be inconclusive
- scientists will keep testing until they become more certain.

4.3 Background information

◆ *The rules of the scientific game – Popper's scientific method*

The classic view of science that we tend to take for granted today comes from Karl Popper's work (Chapter 1). He suggests that science involves:

1. suggesting a hypothesis to explain a phenomenon
2. deducing from the hypothesis that an observable event will occur if the hypothesis is true/false – this is often called making a prediction
3. testing by experiment to establish if the prediction is correct – this is collecting evidence for or against
4. accepting, rejecting or modifying the hypothesis in the light of the evidence.

This is often referred to as the hypothetico-deductive model, or the scientific method (Figure 4.2, after Giere, 1991).

Figure 4.2 *The scientific method*

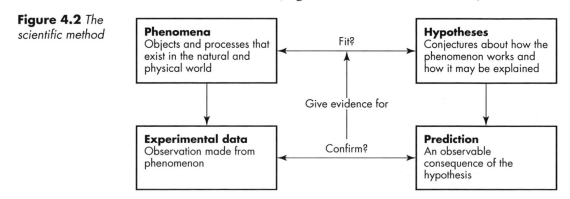

The diagram shows that one 'rule of the game' is that a hypothesis should be confirmed by experimental data. Scientists take results as evidence that the hypothesis is right, or fits the phenomenon. Popper pointed out that evidence can never give final or absolute proof of rightness – all hypotheses should be regarded as potentially wrong, or falsifiable. Hypotheses that cannot be falsified are rejected, as Box 4.1 illustrates. So, in principle, scientific experiments must have the potential to falsify rather than confirm a hypothesis. As successive experiments confirm rather than falsify, a hypothesis gets stronger support, developing into more secure knowledge. In practice, scientists take a positive stance, looking to confirm a hypothesis, rather than a negative, falsifying one trying to find fault. In this model, science can be regarded as a procedure for testing and rejecting hypotheses.

The possibility of being wrong is important to scientific progress. To illustrate this, we give the example of a hypothesis that was proposed but could not be tested as right or wrong in Box 4.1. The example, called the Omphalos hypothesis, is worth discussing with students. The purpose is to show that a good scientific question is open to being found both correct and wrong. In science lessons, we focus almost entirely on describing material that has already been proven or is accepted as true. We forget that behind this lie many ideas and experiments that have never been reported because they yielded data that meant a hypothesis was rejected. Showing both sides of the scientific method coin is more honest.

Box 4.1 The importance of the possibility of being wrong: the Omphalos hypothesis

The Omphalos hypothesis was proposed in 1857 by a well-known naturalist, Philip Henry Gosse (1810–88), who attempted to explain how the Earth was created in his book *Omphalos: An Attempt to Untie the Geological Knot*.
Gosse observed cycles in nature, such as life passing from egg to chicken and from chicken to egg; water flowing from river to sea and from sea to river. At a time when strong literal belief in the Bible was common, Gosse suggested that God started these cycles. So at the moment of creation, organisms looked older than they really were, as if they had existed earlier. God created trees with growth rings, intestines with waste matter in them, teeth with signs of wear and, naturally,

---

Adam and Eve, the Bible's first human beings, with navels (*omphalos* means 'navel' in Greek). Adam and Eve's navels suggested that they had been born, but, Gosse reasoned, they were created by God to look like this. Fossils were thought to have been created and planted by God to imply the Earth was older than it really was. This sounds rather crazy – but Gosse genuinely believed it. Luckily, no one took him seriously and the idea was savagely rejected, to Gosse's dismay.

One main reason for its rejection is that the hypothesis can't be proved wrong – ultimately, the omphalos hypothesis would mean we have no idea how old anything really is, as we could have been created with memory of the past. How could we test the hypothesis by experiment when any data we might collect would also be subject to the same hypothesis? There is no way of collecting reliable evidence – all or none of the evidence could have been generated in one of God's more creative moments just a few seconds earlier. The omphalos hypothesis leads to the conclusion that 'nothing is real' (*Strawberry Fields Forever*, The Beatles, 1967).

◆ *Children's ideas about scientific experiments and scientific questions*

The ideas that 9–16-year-olds have about scientific questions and experiments were investigated in the 1996 research project of Driver and co-workers, discussed in Chapter 3 (pp. 70–73).

What is an experiment?

Children were asked to evaluate which of nine statements about people doing different activities could be classified as an experiment. The statements distinguished between practical activities such as making a cake; following instructions on a worksheet to make a crystal; and evaluation of a hypothesis. Children gave four different types of response:

- ◆ all practical activity can be an experiment
- ◆ an experiment involves making a phenomenon happen, or finding something new
- ◆ an experiment relates cause and effect
- ◆ an experiment involves evaluating a theory.

All practical activity can be an experiment

At the simplest level, children classified any activity that involved practical work as an experiment. This could reflect experiences of school science, in which even the simplest use of practical equipment is usually called an experiment. Younger children tend to make this kind of statement frequently.

An experiment involves making a phenomenon happen, or finding something new

Children may think an experiment means making something new happen, or revealing something new about a phenomenon. Children reasoned that making a cake or a salt crystal could reveal something new if a person had not done this before. The researchers' statement on rain, for example, was:

'This person has a hunch that there is usually more rain in April than in September. They are keeping a diary of the weather each day to see if their hunch is right.' (Driver *et al.*, 1996, p. 86)

In an interview, two 16-year-olds said this was an experiment:

Student 1: … you've got to experiment and see how much rainfall there is, because that's how the weather reporters know it

Student 2: They do it for the weather reports

Interviewer: OK, when you say you have to experiment to figure out, what do you mean by experiment?

Student 1: graphs

Student 2: to see how much it rained

(*op. cit.*, p. 88)

The researchers concluded that students reasoned the unknown nature of the outcome, that is, the finding out of rainfall figures, made the activity an experiment.

Demonstration experiments may also contribute to this reasoning: the outcomes are unknown to children, so are unexpected. Teachers create mystery around the demonstration, indicating that something new will be revealed.

An experiment relates cause and effect

Children may connect the term experiment with doing an investigation, often comparing conditions that affect an outcome. The researchers' statement entitled 'Dissolve' was:

'This person has an idea that the smaller the grains in sugar, the quicker it will dissolve in water, and is testing the idea.'

Around 60% of respondents aged 9–16 indicated that they agreed this was an experiment, probably because this closely reflected the kinds of experiment driven by the UK National Curriculum (DES, 1991) at the time of the research. These involved controlling variables in fair tests.

An experiment involves evaluating a theory

Older children were more likely to view scientific experiments as evaluating a theory. To arrive at this requires deeper thinking than the cause-and-effect discussed above. A student needs to know there is a theory in the background that is being evaluated. For example, the statement entitled 'Balloon' was:

'When the bottle is heated, the balloon fills with air. This could be because the air expands when heated or because hot air rises. This person is heating the bottle upside-down to find out which idea is best.' (*op. cit.*, p. 86)

A 16-year-old said that the second sentence represents theoretical statements that are being evaluated. About 50% of 16-year-olds compared with only 10% of 9-year-olds put this in writing. The researchers found that older students rejected some statements as not representing experiments because there was no theory behind them. An example was the statement 'Towel':

'This person is finding out which one of the three paper towels is best at mopping up water.' (*op. cit.*, p. 86)

This was rejected as being only 'testing an idea', rather than evaluating a theory.

What makes a question scientific?

Children were asked which of 11 suggested questions they regarded as 'scientific'. The questions included some that could be answered by empirical (data-collecting) work and others that could not. 'Is the Earth's atmosphere heating up?' is one empirical question based on a natural phenomenon, while 'Which is the best programme on TV?' can be answered by personal opinion.

The researchers found diverse views, but established three key features of questions that children regard as scientific:

♦ empirical investigation – whether the answer could be obtained empirically, by collecting data or making measurements or observations
♦ natural phenomena – whether or not the question addressed a natural phenomenon
♦ scientists' characteristics – how respondents' personal views of what scientists do and how they work related to the question.

Empirical investigation

Children applied several criteria to establish if a question could be investigated empirically. These mirrored responses given to the statements on science experiments discussed above. For example, children thought that questions such as 'How was the Earth made?', 'Is the Earth's atmosphere heating up?' and 'Which is the best diet to keep babies healthy?' could be answered easily by observation, noting whether or not the phenomenon occurred.

Others related cause and effect: the Earth-heating question generated this response from a 16-year-old at interview:

'You've got to decide what's causing it. If it is heating up, then you've got to try and stop it by using different things like no CFCs ...' (*op. cit.*, p. 76)

A few students looked for an underlying theory in a question. As theories were not mentioned in any questions, this required sophisticated reasoning and, perhaps unsurprisingly, was rare.

The possibility of testing by experiment was a less common response than others: around 30% of 16-year-olds gave this answer as a key criterion for deciding if a question was scientific, compared with fewer than 20% of 9-year-olds and around 20% of 12-year-olds.

Natural phenomena

Children regarded a question as scientific if a natural phenomenon was mentioned or implied. Questions about TV programmes, washing powder and ghosts were generally rejected as non-scientific, while 'Which diet is best to keep babies healthy?', 'Is the Earth's atmosphere heating up?', 'How was the Earth made?' and 'Can any metal be made into a magnet?' were perceived as scientific. Students also distinguished between ethical issues and scientific ones, in this respect matching views held by scientists and other adults. Some questions were identified as scientific on social grounds alone, such as the babies' diet and Earth origin questions:

'... so they [babies] don't get diarrhoea all the time'

'We need to stop pollution destroying it [the Earth]' (*op. cit.*, p. 81)

Certain issues seemed to stand out as being scientific due to media popularity. These related to child health and global warming. Other issues that were not so popular could be either scientific or non-scientific, for different reasons. The question 'Can any metal be made into a magnet?' is not a social issue, so students were not primed to view this in a scientific way because of media influence.

Scientists' characteristics

Children's stereotypes of scientists were apparent. Some 9-year-olds, for example, rejected 'Which diet is best to keep babies healthy?' because scientists would not 'bother with babies' food and things like that' (*op. cit.*, p. 82); and 'Is it cheaper to buy a large or a small packet of washing powder?' because '... if they've got wives, their wives will be doing it' (*op. cit.*, p. 82).

Older children referred to scientists' professional interests, addressing socially important questions. They also perceived scientists as working collaboratively and in different kinds of settings.

Children's ideas about experiments and scientific questions – key points

Children's ideas reflect a combination of social and school-based knowledge. In school science, 'experiment' describes all practical activity, however complex and whether or not the outcome is known beforehand. Children investigate the temperature at which water boils as an experiment, even though they know the result, or even if they do not know, they are aware that the teacher knows. The 'deceit' of passing off a descriptive test as an experiment is widely practised.

Topics that receive media attention, such as child health and climate change, are seen as scientific, even for non-scientific reasons. Other scientific topics that don't receive this attention can be seen as either scientific or non-scientific.

Few 9–16-year-olds connect experiment to theory, a basic component of scientific method. Any understanding of scientific method and the role of experiments in making discoveries or establishing new knowledge is limited.

We encourage development of children's thinking along these lines:

♦ science often involves thinking of hypotheses that can be tested by experiments that will produce evidence
♦ a good hypothesis must be answerable 'true' or 'false' by experiment
♦ evidence obtained by experiment has to be interpreted
♦ evidence can generate new hypotheses that are then tested
♦ evidence contributes to scientific discoveries.

In the activities section, we suggest how to help children understand these points.

4.4 Summary

This chapter emphasises the importance of evidence and experiments in how science works. We show that evidence can result in a hypothesis being accepted or rejected, but also can require further evidence for confirmation or rejection.

Children's ideas show a range of different viewpoints based on their mixing school and everyday knowledge. By combining the activities and key points above, we hope teachers will be able to draw out specific aspects of science relating to experiments and the role of evidence to help address misconceptions.

4.5 References and resources

Driver, R., Leach, J., Millar, R. and Scott, P. (1996) *Young People's Images of Science*. Buckingham: Open University Press.
Department for Education and Science/Welsh Office (DES/WO) (1991) *Science in the National Curriculum*. London: HMSO.
Giere, R.N. (1991) *Understanding Scientific Reasoning 3rd edition*. Fort Worth Tx: Holt, Rinehart and Winston.

Louis Agassiz and the global Ice Age
Biographies of Agassiz can be found at:
  www.ucmp.berkeley. edu/history/agassiz.html
  http://academic.emporia.edu/aberjame/histgeol/agassiz/agassiz.htm
Charles Lyell is well represented on the web, for example at:
  www.victorianweb.org/science/lyell.html
  www.mnsu.edu/emuseum/information/biography/klmno/lyell_charles.html

The real cause of stomach ulcers
Barry Marshall and J. Robin Warren's work is described very well on the Nobel Prize website at http://nobelprize.org/nobel_ prizes/medicine/laureates/2005/press.html
This website gives a biography of Barry Marshall and includes an excellent image of the bacterium *H. pylori*:
  www.achievement.org/autodoc/page/mar1bio-1
This is a short biography of J. Robin Warren: www.nndb.com/people/342/000136931

The case of the Martian stone
This is the best website with information about this case:
www2.jpl.nasa.gov/snc/nasa1.html
A website with this story and others about Mars exploration is:
www.spacetoday.org/SolSys/Mars/MarsThePlanet/MarsRocks
.html

The Omphalos hypothesis
Gosse's book describing the Omphalos hypothesis is reviewed
here: www.burgy.50megs.com/omphalos.htm
This general website gives a very clear introduction to
Omphalos: www.answers.com/topic/omphalos-theology

Creativity

5.1 Why do you need this chapter?

The aims of this chapter are to:

♦ show that creativity in science plays a key role in making
scientific discoveries
♦ discuss aspects of creativity in science that do not normally
receive attention
♦ suggest that students' creativity in science can be developed.

Almost every day, we hear of a new scientific development – in
the news recently, for example, was a method of treating
degenerative eye disease by grafting unaffected cells from
within the eye (http://news.bbc.co.uk/1/hi/health/
6722435.stm). Where do such developments come from?
Someone with expertise in grafting cells and knowledge of the
eye must have had an idea that this could work, and driven a
project to this conclusion. Describing how this happens is the
purpose of this book – and creativity is a special factor that
helps drive scientific progress. Creative thinking, perhaps
drawing information from several different sources, must have
played a role.

So, in meeting the first two aims, we want to show that
creativity in science means more than connecting science with
arts subjects – projects such as writing poems or plays about
scientific topics, representing science through dance, or similar.
These are worthy activities, but we think creativity deserves
attention from a different angle. In the Background information
section (page 99), we give a definition of creativity and discuss
the topic from the perspectives of chance, logic, *zeitgeist* (spirit of
the age) and genius. Einstein described scientists as 'people with
a passion to know'. Creativity lies at the heart of that passion.

Activities based on creativity are provided. These take
unusual approaches. At their root is the notion that we can
train students' creativity. Doing this may bring benefits, such as
the ability to handle a wider range of information and
situations more easily, and the ability to solve problems and to

become more resilient learners, able to cope with difficulties. The workplace for students we teach today is likely to be different from our own – more flexible working and different styles of workplace are likely. Developing creativity skills may mean they can handle their future more easily.

These are ambitious aims that are slightly aside from the science National Curriculum. Nevertheless, we think this is an important chapter – scientific progress depends on creative scientists having ideas. How science works undeniably involves creativity.

5.2 Activities

Three activities are suggested:

♦ using your creativity
♦ chemical egg races
♦ the link between smoking and lung cancer.

♦ *Using your creativity*

Time required: about 30 minutes for each of four questions
NC link: 1b, c, 2a

Learning outcomes
Starter: Snow on the line

Invite the class to brainstorm a solution to the following situation.

In north-west Canada one winter, a very severe snowfall blocked the main railway line in a remote area. If the situation was not resolved, food supplies in some settlements that relied on the railway further down the line would not get through. For workers to reach the area to unblock the line from the nearest settlement would take several days walking through mountains. What could be done to solve the problem?

The rules for brainstorming suggest that each person is asked for an answer, or they may say 'pass'. Possible solutions are recorded and then the best few are discussed.

The solution to this apocryphal situation is that helicopters were used to blow the snow off the lines. Why they could not have been used to fly resources to cut-off villages was not explained!

Main activity

We suggest four alternative questions. Each could be used in a connected topic, such as Earth and space, forces, or investigations and technology-related areas. The tasks are taken from a creativity test in science devised by Hu and Adey (2002). The tasks may not appear particularly original, but the point is that each one is open-ended. The first three, Space, Gravity and Napkins, all have the important quality of variety – asking for a range of methods or viewpoints. The ability to come up with many different suggestions is regarded as a key indicator for high levels of creativity. If these do not appeal or fit with your topics, we suggest alternative sources for open-ended situations on page 111)

Space

If you could take a spaceship to travel in outer space and go to a planet, what scientific questions would you want to research? List as many as you can.

Gravity

Suppose there was no gravity – describe what the world would be like.

Napkins

There are two kinds of napkin – how can you test which is better? Write down as many possible methods as you can and the instruments, principles and simple procedures you would follow.

Apple-picking machine

Design an apple-picking machine. Draw a picture of your machine, labelling the parts with their names and functions.

Running the activity

Start by asking students to come up with their own ideas first, thinking individually for some time, before pooling ideas in a pair or group and sparking from each other to come up with original suggestions.

Depending on how much time you wish to allow, the Napkins and Apple-picking machine tasks could be extended to actually doing the experiments or building the machine from scrap materials. Napkins is a classic investigation-type task. The apple-picking machine could provide a good link to technological developments. For information about how James Dyson invented the bagless vacuum cleaner, see www.dyson.co.uk → About Dyson → The Dyson Story, which describes the observation that led to the development. The Space task could be related to space missions going to distant planets, such as the Cassini–Huygens mission to Saturn (http://saturn.jpl.nasa.gov). The gravity task could be related to experiences of weightlessness described by astronauts, and experiments carried out on the International Space Station (see http://www.nasa.gov → Missions → Current missions → International Space Station.

Plenary discussion

- Draw out the variation in solutions to the tasks.
- Indicate that there is no single, 'correct' solution.
- Point out that scientists often have to solve problems by coming up with creative solutions – scientists may suggest different ways of solving the same problem.
- Ask students to suggest other factors that also influence how scientists make scientific discoveries.
- If possible, make connections between the students' suggestions and those of scientists working in real life, using the suggestions above.

◆ *Chemical egg races*

Time required: 2 hours
NC link: 2a, 2b, 2c

Learning outcomes

This activity has its origins in the 1980s, when chemical egg racing was popular. The sport developed from a TV programme, *The Great Egg Race*, which ran from 1978 to 1986. The programme challenged teams of university scientists to make gadgets from limited resources to meet a specific need, such as to support someone's weight, bridge a river, and so on. The classic weekly task was to construct a machine to transport an egg as far as possible. The principle of solving open-ended tasks using simple resources was adapted by chemists, generating chemical egg races. A chemical egg race involves setting an open-ended problem-solving task for students. The thrill lies in making this competitive and time-limited, with a prize for the best solution. Eggs don't usually play a part – but working in teams and devising novel ways of solving a problem within a specified time limit are constant factors.

The Royal Society of Chemistry has published two books of problems suitable for chemical egg races (see page 111). Both are available online in pdf format.

Organising an egg race

Prior experiences of egg-racing suggest that this is an extremely enjoyable activity that creates an excellent atmosphere. Students quickly become hooked on the idea and really work hard to generate good solutions.

Pre-planning

◆ Ensure all materials are available, with spare items.
◆ Organise students into teams before the lesson.
◆ If prizes are involved, perhaps have an independent judge watching the lesson to decide who gets them.
◆ Consider making a video for future publicity.
◆ Consider competing with students from one or more other schools. This can have a positive effect on students' behaviour.
◆ Consider Chemistry Week (www.rsc.org) or National Science and Engineering Week (www.the-ba.net) as a good occasion for running an egg race.

On the day

◆ Depending on the task, build in time for students to demonstrate their solutions. If time is short, run the egg race over two lessons – one for preparation and the next for demonstration.
◆ Keep to strict time limits.
◆ To emphasise the creative aspect, ensure the prize goes to the team with the most novel and inventive solution.

Plenary discussion

To emphasise creativity, following the egg race ask students to reflect on the skills they used to solve the problem. Try to identify the role of creativity in coming up with a novel solution. The following questions may make good discussion points.

◆ What makes a good team?
◆ Is it easy or difficult to produce solutions? Why?
◆ Are some people naturally better at this kind of task? Can people learn to do these tasks?
◆ Why is solving problems a good skill to have?

Usually a team needs a good mixture of skills, rather than people who have the same skills. The mixture enables sharing of ideas, which can lead to a novel solution. Some people seem to be naturally good at producing a lot of ideas, others may have just one or two, but these can be very good. Students can realise that the quietest team member may be the one to make the key contribution. With practice, people can get better at solving open-ended problems. This is similar to learning to solve Sudoku, cryptic crosswords and other puzzles. Problem-solving is a valuable skill that is often required in the workplace.

◆ *The link between smoking and lung cancer*

Time required: About 40 minutes
NC link: 1b, 3a

Learning outcomes
The link between smoking and lung cancer was made first in 1954 by doctors Richard Doll and Bradford Hill. This activity encourages students to use logical deductions from their original data to reach a conclusion. The activity includes an interview with Richard Doll published shortly before he died in 2005.

Running the activity
Students will require copies of the fact sheet and the three data tables and the interview on the CD task sheet. Students can work together or individually.

Answers to questions

1. a) 87%
   b) 55–64 and 65–74
   c) 45–54 and 55–64
   d) About the same – no real change.
2. a) Heart attack, lung cancer, other heart diseases.
   b) Probably because lung cancer was the only cause of death not seen among non-smokers – this suggested a link.
   c) Heart disease, heart attack.
3. a) Thirteen heavy smokers actually died from lung cancer, compared with only seven who would have been expected to die from lung cancer if there was no link.
   b) In a way, this was quite weak evidence – based on only a few men. But statistically the data were significant, so the figures should have been taken more seriously.

4. a) The Government claimed that smoking could not be formally identified as a cause of lung cancer.
    b) The tobacco industry claimed that air pollution was responsible for lung cancer.
    c) They did not want to scare people unnecessarily or put tobacco companies' profits at risk.
    d) Nicotine is highly addictive and it is hard to break this addiction.
5. Smoking is now known to contribute to other cancers such as mouth and throat cancers, low birth-weight babies and other problems in pregnancy, and heart disease/higher risk of heart attack.

Plenary discussion

♦ It will probably be easy to become side-tracked onto smoking issues, but the point here is really to show that logic plays a part in making scientific discoveries. People are often slow to catch on – where logic is involved, ideas can be difficult to understand. This could have contributed to the slow response to the findings. We tend either to panic about logical conclusions, as in the cases of bovine spongiform encephalopathy (BSE) and the measles, mumps and rubella (MMR) vaccine – or fail to understand the consequences, as happened here.

♦ *What makes a genius?*

Time required: About an hour maximum
NC link: 3c

We don't normally think of great scientists as being alive – usually children only learn about dead scientists, mostly men from the nineteenth century. This activity provides an opportunity for students to find out more about some of the UK's best living scientists. They will learn about their work, their lives, and factors that have contributed to their success. Some of those listed are already well known, others less so. The fact sheet on the CD provides basic background information and websites to access for further information. This article from *The Independent* provides background reading: http://education.independent.co.uk/higher/article2904373.ece. The article highlights the role genius scientists play in developing new knowledge.

Running the activity

Ten scientists are listed in the table on the CD. Some have won Nobel Prizes, others are well known in their field.

♦ Divide the class into small groups – pairs will probably work best.
♦ Each pair needs access to ICT facilities.
♦ Students research the scientists listed. Questions are provided on the task sheet on the CD.
♦ Students could be asked to present their findings relating to one or more scientists in a plenary session.

Plenary discussion

Draw out the following points.

♦ Does the information indicate that there are factors that contribute to scientists becoming successful? If so, what are these?
♦ Do you have to be a genius to be a good scientist?
♦ What influence do the best scientists have? Why are they important?

5.3 Background information

♦ *Defining creativity*

We define creativity as 'the ability to produce novel and appropriate work' (Sternberg and Lubart, 1999). Applying this to science, we take 'novel and appropriate' to mean new discoveries that have an impact on our understanding and experience of the natural world.

♦ *Chance*

Chance plays a role in making scientific discoveries. Scientists cannot plan to find something novel – rather, by working systematically and knowledgeably on a topic, they put themselves in a strong position to take advantage of a chance event. The chance event, such as Henri Becquerel discovering his fogged photographic plates that were placed next to radioactive material, provides the source of new and appropriate work.

The biologist Louis Pasteur (1822–95) said in a lecture in 1854: 'In the field of observation, chance favours only the prepared mind'. A common misunderstanding is that discoveries made by chance could have been made by anyone, and that there is nothing special about them. This is not the case – scientists who have made chance discoveries have all been active, conscientious, determined, diligent and clever.

A good example is Alexander Fleming's work on the *Penicillium* mould that led to the development of antibiotics. The story goes that, although a brilliant researcher, Fleming was chaotic about his laboratory organisation. He returned from holiday in September 1928 to find that some bacterial culture plates were contaminated with mould, and threw them into disinfectant. The arrival of a visitor interested in his research prompted Fleming to rescue plates that had almost become submerged. He showed the plates to the visitor, noticing clear zones around the mouldy areas in which bacteria could not grow. Fleming kept the plates, then isolated a substance he called 'penicillin' from the mould.

Closer inspection of this incident suggests that Fleming was not just lucky – there was more to his discovery than chance alone. His past experiences of working with bacterial cultures prompted him to investigate the clear zones, knowing that these were unusual. He must have had excellent knowledge to realise the significance of the observation, and the experimental skills necessary to extract the active agent. Although he was not looking for antibiotics, Fleming's creative abilities enabled him to exploit the opportunity that chance offered.

The term 'serendipity' is often applied to scientific discoveries made by chance. Keith Simonton, an American psychologist, defines this (perhaps somewhat obviously) as 'making fortunate discoveries by accident' (Simonton, 2004, p. 8). Fact sheet Serendipitous discoveries (on the CD) lists some discoveries made through serendipitous events over several centuries. These can have a disproportionately large effect on scientific history, even becoming part of science folklore. Isaac Newton 'discovering gravity' through the chance event of an apple falling on his head while sitting under an apple tree is one example. Box 5.1 describes the truth behind this myth.

Box 5.1 Newton, gravity and the apple

Question: Is it true that Newton discovered gravity when an apple fell on his head while sat under an apple tree?

Newton worked on the ideas that went into *Principia Mathematica* for more than 20 years. From 1665–66, England was ravaged by bubonic plague. Newton, then in his early twenties, avoided infection by returning to live in the country at Woolsthorpe, near Grantham in Lincolnshire, where he had grown up. The orchard there is the supposed site of the apple fall. Newton is said to have confirmed the story to his biographer William Stukeley in 1726, while they were walking together under apple trees in the garden of his London home:

> '... amidst other discourse, he told me, he was in the same situation as when formerly the notion of gravitation came into his mind. It was occasioned by the fall of an apple, as he sat in the contemplative mood.' (Stukeley, quoted by White, 1998, p. 86)

The French philosopher Voltaire mentioned the apple story as coming from Newton's niece, a lady called Mrs Conduitt:

> 'One day in the year 1666, Newton, having returned to the country and seeing the fruits of a tree fall, fell ... into a deep meditation about the cause that thus attracts bodies in the line which, if produced, would pass nearly through the centre of the Earth.' (Voltaire, quoted by White, 1998, p. 86)

We like this story because it is easy to understand, contributing to a soothing image of Newton as a 'genius scientist' able to transform simple events into great scientific principles. However, closer inspection of Newton's papers (White, 1998, p. 92–93) shows that the story was probably concocted by Newton himself as a way of covering up, or perhaps simplifying for the benefit of the public, his struggle with understanding gravity. The experience in Woolsthorpe orchard probably happened and provided some inspiration, but the development of the law of gravity arose from the collection and analysis of a great deal of experimental evidence over a 20-year period.

Answer: No.

Chance also plays a role in solving problems requiring insight. These problems cannot be solved only by applying logic. Like riddles, they require understanding of a 'trick' or 'catch' to arrive at a solution. Newton applied the trick of his new law of universal gravitation to arrive at the idea that planets orbit the Sun in the same way a cannonball travels when fired. Arriving at solutions to difficult problems, insight often involves a scientist putting the problem on the mental 'back-burner' for weeks, months or even years while doing more work. Their work involves mentally turning over different ideas, perhaps from a range of projects, and being exposed to everyday events, even mundane news stories. The solution is produced when a combination of ideas comes together to produce the required trick. Archimedes's *'Eureka!'* ('I have found it!') moment is a good example: bathing provided the solution to the problem of finding the volume and hence the density of an irregular object, the new crown made for the King of Syracuse, in order to determine if it was made from solid gold or a combination of gold and lesser-value metals. Intuition rather than logic is the important key factor in these events.

Insight suggests that scientists are always working towards one 'correct' solution, but this is not really the case. As earlier chapters indicate, we are used to looking back at what has already been discovered, viewing science from the perspective of what is agreed and/or confirmed knowledge. We imitate this in science lessons, describing or asking children to repeat outcomes of experiments, even though the result is already known. Chance can play no part – the outcomes are predetermined. This does not imitate how science works in practice. It is more realistic to think in terms of creative production. Scientists work on problems that are genuinely open-ended, with no obvious solution. To help students realise and experience this, the first activity stimulates creativity (see page 93). If we want to imitate creativity in real life, we need to provide genuine open-ended problems producing creative products. Group creativity, involving brainstorming, can be useful to help arrive at solutions to these. The most productive science research groups tend to be those where overlapping skills and interests are apparent, but in which different viewpoints and ideas can be expressed. Chance plays a major role when the unexpected combination of ideas from two or more similar, but different, scientists leads to new creative products and solutions to seemingly intractable problems.

◆ *Logic*

Science has long been regarded as a logical subject, beginning with the philosopher Francis Bacon (see Chapter 1). The hypothetico-deductive method of doing science (see Chapter 4), involving logical steps of proposing, testing and then rejecting, accepting or refining theories, is thought to be the best, most assured route to scientific discovery. This is on the basis that logical deductions fit the facts, so scientific 'truth' emerges that cannot be disputed.

One school of thought takes this to extremes, suggesting that by understanding the logic involved in any field of science, creativity in terms of new discoveries is assured. In 1973, the psychologist Herbert Simon proposed that scientific creativity is nothing more than problem-solving, and is controlled entirely by logical procedures. He based his reasoning partly on work using computer programs to simulate the logical steps involved in making famous scientific discoveries. Simon argues that if a discovery can be imitated by a computer, then practically anyone can make an important contribution to science.

Simon's views may be true up to a point – much of what scientists do is to work on day-to-day puzzle-solving (see Thomas Kuhn, Chapter 1), rather like solving the crossword puzzle in a daily newspaper: once readers get into the way a compiler works, they can adopt stepwise solutions and use routines to arrive at answers to individual clues, creating strategies for more difficult ones. Similarly, scientists learn the rules, theories, facts, experimental techniques, equations and other information relating to their field, and work on problems within their area of interest, keeping closely to accepted paradigms. Each puzzle solved is a creative contribution in itself. A few will make truly ground-breaking discoveries in the course of a career, while others will have high-impact ideas that help to develop the field in new ways.

Application of logic alone cannot be the only route to major new creative work in science. As we saw above, some problems cannot be solved solely by application of logic – they require application of an extra step, a catch or trick, in order to be resolved. In this situation, scientists may apply logical steps, such as breaking down the problem into smaller parts then solving each one in turn; finding an analogy to obtain an alternative picture; or resorting to trial and error. Even then, some problems simply resist solution, such as when serious anomalies arise in puzzle-solving science. The mass increase measured by Antoine Lavoisier on the formation of mercury(II) oxide is an example, as this contradicted the phlogiston theory (a seventeenth-century attempt to explain oxidation processes such as fire and rusting). Resolution could not be achieved by logic applied from within the accepted theoretical framework. Chance (see above) and genius (see below) both contributed to the resolution of this problem and the establishment of a new explanation for combustion.

Overall, logic provides a basic framework within which science operates, constraining the creative process in three main ways.

♦ Information in the pool used by scientists must be logical, not contravening basic laws such as the conservation of energy, conservation of mass, etc. Arguments based on 'small green aliens', miracles or other supernatural phenomena cannot be sustained by logic.

♦ Logic limits the range of possible combinations of ideas from material within the pool. This is because science knowledge is interconnected. New combinations creating a solution to a problem cannot always be generated at random. This is similar to the constraints applied to gene combinations – the closer together two genes are on a chromosome, the less freedom they have to recombine in a new way. Scientists have to look outside the field to find powerful new combinations of ideas that help solve difficult problems.

♦ Logic applies to outcomes of the creative process – 'does this hang together?' is always the issue with a new discovery. That is, are basic tenets of science contravened? Does the new idea, theory or discovery survive logical arguments levelled against it? In the end, science is upheld by application of internal logical reasoning that determines the truth of new findings.

Given this framework of logic, creative scientists tend to work on several projects at once, with different levels of risk. High-risk projects have the potential to make great contributions, but may require solutions to insight problems (see page 99) that appear to defy logic and hence take time to solve. Low-risk projects are of the puzzle-solving variety that keep scientists ticking over in terms of creativity, each generating a new contribution to the field without inducing radical change.

♦ Zeitgeist: the spirit of the age

From the *zeitgeist* perspective, scientific discoveries are products of the environment in which scientists work. Sociologists call this the socio-cultural system. Taking this view, discoveries and new ideas are in the air and ripe for picking by scientists as inevitable outcomes of their work. Stem cell research receives a lot of attention at the moment – this is a fashionable area of science commanding funding and expertise. This is an example of *zeitgeist* within biology. Discoveries resulting from stem cell research are likely to multiply in the future.

Evidence that *zeitgeist* has a role in scientific creativity comes from the occasions when discoveries have been made by two or more people at about the same time. Fact sheet Multiple discoveries (on the CD) gives examples. These arise from developments within a specific science. Scientists work from a pool of available material, comprising knowledge that is agreed and accepted, as well as ideas that are being worked on. Alongside this are social issues, such as the desire to improve the health of a population, preserve national security in war, or handle global climate change. Scientists combine (implicitly or explicitly) material from the pool and context to develop new ideas and make discoveries. If sufficient numbers of scientists are involved, then multiple discoveries are inevitable – active, lively conditions for research provide the environment within which more than one scientist can make the same discovery.

Evidence for *zeitgeist* playing a major role in scientific creativity is weak. Closer inspection reveals that many so-called multiple discoveries are more different than they are alike. Scientists making the same discovery combine ideas from within and outside the available information independently of each other. They make the same discovery, but use different routes. Discoveries arise not through *zeitgeist*, but by chance. An example well known to physicists is the discovery in the seventeenth century of the mathematical procedures involved in calculus by both Isaac Newton and Gottfried Leibniz. This became a major controversy, both scientists claiming its invention independently, through different routes. A more recent example is the independent and simultaneous observation of nuclear magnetic resonance (NMR) in 1946, by scientists at Harvard and Stanford Universities on the east and west coasts of the USA, respectively. When scientists from the two groups met, Edward Purcell of Harvard (who later shared the 1952 Nobel Prize with Felix Bloch from Stanford) said: 'It was an hour before either of us understood how the other was trying to explain it' (quoted by Simonton, 2004, p. 37). This suggests that although the outcome was the same, the two groups had discovered NMR by different routes. Research on many of the examples listed in the Fact sheet reveals similar patterns – what appears to be exact coincidence is really scientists working independently in the same area coming up with similar results.

If *zeitgeist* were really significant in making new discoveries, we would see many more examples of the same discovery being made by the same or a very similar route, but this is extremely rare. Darwin's and Wallace's development of the theory of evolution by natural selection is the only one known. In this instance, Darwin and Wallace announced evolution in a joint paper, with Darwin taking the lead later. In most of the examples listed in Fact sheet Multiple discoveries, disputes occurred between scientists claiming the discoveries. Joseph Priestley went to the opposite extreme, refusing to accept the significance of his discovery and persisting with his belief in phlogiston. A more realistic position is to think of *zeitgeist* as providing three factors that support scientific creativity:

♦ a means of communicating and disseminating information through conferences, journals and learned societies
♦ a collection of material, theories, ideas, equations, phenomena, and so on that scientists can draw on for their work
♦ a sense of agreement about which problems should attract the most research effort.

Zeitgeist is useful in explaining features of the era within which scientists work: it is not a cause or source of scientific discovery or creativity. A new discovery is not inevitable – even given the right conditions, chance must play a part. For example, the DNA double helix would almost certainly have been discovered if the productive partnership of Francis Crick and James Watson had not hit on the solution – but by a very different route, perhaps taking several more years and involving the contributions of a larger number of scientists working in the biological *zeitgeist* of the 1950s.

♦ *The scientific genius*

Geniuses have a particular role in making scientific discoveries. These people show extreme creativity in their ability to produce new ideas. They have an extensive range of mental strategies available, including the ability to combine ideas and information from different areas, ignoring the usual logical pathways of scientific method, taking advantage of the *zeitgeist* and consequently being well prepared to see the potential in chance events. Psychologists suggest that genius scientists make unusual associations and analogies, as well as using rich, dream-like imagery. Other qualities include having a very high IQ (intelligence quotient) score of 135 or above (a feature particular to science geniuses but not always found in geniuses in other fields), a powerful memory, and the ability to work on a range of projects at once.

Fact sheet Geniuses (on the CD) illustrates these points using a small selection of famous genius scientists. The table (based on data from Cox, 1926) is organised by posthumous (possibly over-)estimates of the scientists' IQ values. It is rather tongue-in-cheek, not intended as a really serious piece of information, but as a point of interest. We suggest each scientist's most famous discovery, and indicate other fields to which they contributed. The IQ values range from 135 (Faraday) to 190 (Pascal). An IQ of around 135 is, for the statistically minded, two standard deviations above the average IQ value for the population. For the non-statistically minded, this means that very few people have an IQ this high, and even fewer a value of 150 or over. Interestingly, Faraday, the lowest ranked, was known for his competence as an experimental scientist rather than a theoretical one; his mathematical skills were poor. Frenchman Blaise Pascal's IQ is estimated at 190, an enormously high value: he contributed significantly in a wide range of fields, including work on pressure (the SI unit of pressure is named 'Pascal' after him). Examples of geniuses' ability to generate new ideas without evidence are shown: William Harvey described mammalian fertilisation 200 years before any evidence was produced. This led to his being called the 'father of embryology'. Lavoisier noted that carbon exists in different forms long before this could be proved. The final column of Fact sheet Geniuses, indicating the wide range of fields to which these men contributed, is perhaps characteristic of the intellectual freedom they enjoyed as well as their exceptional abilities.

Genius is independent of social class and birth status: tenacity and the drive to work on ideas are essential genius qualities. William Harvey and Charles Darwin, for example, were born into wealthy, educated families and attended Cambridge University. In contrast, Michael Faraday was the self-educated son of a London blacksmith who fought to become an assistant to the scientist Humphrey Davy at London's Royal Institution. Isaac Newton was born into a relatively poor farming family in Lincolnshire and educated at village schools. An expensive, formal education or inheriting wealth does not guarantee genius, but may bring advantages by providing background knowledge and experiences. Darwin's father, for example, exasperated by his son's career failures in medicine and the church, paid for Charles's passage as naturalist on *HMS Beagle*. Newton was encouraged by his teachers to stay at school rather than help his mother on the farm. He consequently attended Cambridge University and began his stunning academic career. Faraday could not afford to buy books and had little formal education, presenting himself to Davy out of self-interest and ambition, rather than as the result of parental or other patronage.

Genius is still apparent today among scientists. To help illustrate this, Fact sheet What makes you a genius scientist (on the CD) details some UK-born scientists in different fields who are active researchers and whose contributions may lead to them being regarded as geniuses. Box 5.2 describes Stephen Hawking, probably the best known living scientist recognised as a genius. There are of course women geniuses – but not many in science. Below we offer some discussion that may be helpful in addressing the 'gender issue' with students in school.

Box 5.2 A modern-day scientific genius – Stephen Hawking

Stephen Hawking was born on 8 January 1942 in Oxford, a city the family thought was safer in wartime than London, where they lived. His father, Frank, was a research biologist. He grew up in St Albans, a town about 20 miles north of London, doing well but not exceptionally so at school. Hawking then went to Oxford University, where he gained a first-class honours degree in physics, not doing very much work but being acknowledged as cleverer than most of the lecturers. Doctorate work in cosmology at Cambridge University followed and, after a period of postdoctoral research, Hawking was appointed Lucasian Professor of Mathematics in 1979, 310 years after Isaac Newton held the post. His work on the fundamental laws governing our Universe led to the realisation that space and time began with the Big Bang and will end with black holes. The implications of his work meant that general relativity and quantum theory needed to be unified. A consequence of this unification was the proposal that black holes are not entirely black, but emit radiation and will eventually evaporate. Hawking's work also led to the conjecture that the Universe is unlimited in space and time, so is entirely governed by the laws of science.

In about 1963, Stephen Hawking was found to have an incurable, degenerative illness diagnosed as amyotropic lateral sclerosis, a form of motor neurone disease. Subsequent declines in his physical health mean that he is now confined to a wheelchair as a quadriplegic, speaking through a voice synthesiser. The illness has not prevented him from having a family – he has three children and a grandchild. In April 2007 he took a zero-gravity flight that enabled him to experience weightlessness, floating free of his wheelchair. Of this experience he said: 'Many people have asked me why I am taking this flight. I am doing it for many reasons. First of all, I believe that life on Earth is at an ever increasing risk of being wiped out by a disaster such as sudden global warming, nuclear war, a genetically engineered virus, or other dangers. I think the human race has no future if it doesn't go into space. I therefore want to encourage public interest in space.'

Women geniuses

Naming female geniuses, and female genius scientists, is difficult. If we take the award of a Nobel Prize as an indication of genius, the Nobel laureates Marie Curie and Dorothy Hodgkin come to mind, but others are more difficult. There are many possible reasons for this, including the classic feminist argument that women have been denied equal opportunities with men in work, financial support and education throughout history. We cannot do full justice to this issue here, but raise discussion more specifically as to why women have contributed less in science than in other fields.

The fact sheet (on the CD) lists all female Nobel Prize-winners. It shows that women have won more prizes in literature and peace than in physics, chemistry and physiology or medicine. Only three Nobel Prizes in science have been awarded to female sole winners – Marie Curie (1911), Dorothy Hodgkin (1964) and Barbara McClintock (1983). In contrast, literature and peace prizes have been won a number of times by individual women. No women have won the mathematics or economics prizes. This suggests, tentatively, that women are more successful as politicians and writers than as scientists or abstract thinkers. One possible reason may be that, although the average IQ for men and women is the same, women's IQ values tend to be less broadly distributed than those for men. Consequently, assuming high IQ is a contributory factor to genius, proportionately more men than women will attain this level. A second point is that success in 'hard' sciences requires years of dedicated, laborious work in laboratories and collaboration with colleagues. In the past, these circumstances have not welcomed women. Rosalind Franklin (the X-ray crystallographer who proposed a double helix structure for DNA from her pictures before Crick and Watson hit on the idea) worked at King's College, London in the 1950s. Being female, she was banned from the social environment of the college's 'long room', so could not engage in the productive after-dinner discussion that her male colleagues took for granted. Her reputation as an English 'blue-stocking' reluctant to share her work with others is perhaps unsurprising and unfair, as she was denied full participation in the scientific community. Assuming this experience to be typical, the lack of women genius scientists may arise because fewer women than men actually want to be scientists. Able women find social reform, literature and politics more inviting and accepting of their talents. However, some men and women achieve greatness and high status in science despite lacking privilege, patronage and even formal education. These exceptional people are driven by their ideas and tenacity to contribute despite everything.

5.4 Summary

The drive among scientists to produce new discoveries is extremely strong. For most, this is satisfied by working mainly within one area, contributing new solutions to puzzle-solving tasks by application of logic. The area of work may be controlled to some extent by *zeitgeist* – the social context determining what is critical to the time. Each new discovery can be regarded as a creative contribution, as it resulted from solving an open-ended task, the solution to which was unknown. Chance plays its role when factors come together unexpectedly.

A few genius scientists will make major, ground-breaking contributions that revolutionise our thinking. This group of people work in ways that often defy logic, showing the ability to combine ideas from different areas and produce the trick that resolves a major anomaly, or solves a long-standing problem. Chance plays a stronger role here, but favours those who can hold a multitude of ideas in their heads at once, so that they are able to take advantage of the random observation that provides the final clue.

In school science, giving children the opportunity to be genuinely creative generates stimulating lessons full of surprise.

5.5 References and resources

Cox, C.M. (1926) *The Early Mental Traits of Three Hundred Geniuses*. Stanford, CA: Stanford University Press.

Davies, K. (1990) *In Search of Solutions*. London: Royal Society of Chemistry.

Hu, W. and Adey, P. (2002) A scientific creativity test for secondary school students. *International Journal of Science Education* 24: 389–403.

Simonton, D.K. (2004) *Creativity in Science*. Cambridge: Cambridge University Press.

Sternberg, R.J. and Lubart, T.I. (1999) The concept of creativity: prospects and paradigms. In: Sternberg, R.J. (ed.), *Handbook of Creativity*. Cambridge: Cambridge University Press, pp. 3–15.

Taylor, J. (1993) *In Search of More Solutions*. London: Royal Society of Chemistry.

White, M. (1998) *Isaac Newton, The Last Sorcerer.* London: Fourth Estate.

General resources to help with creativity tasks

The James Dyson website has some interesting links to technological developments: www.dyson.co.uk

The Cassini–Huygens mission to Saturn is featured at: http://saturn.jpl.nasa.gov/home/index.cfm

Experiments carried out on the International Space Station are described at: www.nasa.gov/mission_pages/station/main/index.html

Chemical egg-race problems

Davies, K. (1990) *In Search of Solutions: Some Ideas for Chemical Egg Races and Other Problem-Solving Ideas in Chemistry*. London: Royal Society of Chemistry. www.chemsoc.org/pdf/LearnNet/rsc/ISOS_all.pdf

The link between smoking and lung cancer

Richard Doll's life and work is summarised at: http://news.bbc.co.uk/1/hi/health/3826939.stm

Doll, R. and Hill, A.B. (1954) The mortality of doctors in relation to their smoking habits: a preliminary report. *British Medical Journal* ii: 1451–5 – his original article, available at: www.bmj.com/cgi/reprint/328/7455/1529

Genius scientists and the special role they play in developing new knowledge is discussed in this article in *The Independent*: http://education.independent.co.uk/higher/article2904373.ece

Stephen Hawking's website is: www.hawking.org.uk

The Nobel Foundation's website includes many excellent essays describing prize-winners' achievements: http://nobelprize.org

Ethics

6.1 Why do you need this chapter?

The aims of this chapter are to:

♦ consider that scientific discoveries have advantages and disadvantages
♦ help students understand the ethics behind scientific work
♦ illustrate that science is not always what it seems.

The first aim takes the usual angle on science ethics presented in many published materials. In this version, we present four scientific topics that generate dilemmas for our society. The advantages associated with each topic are clear, but disadvantages are also apparent. Our emphasis is on examining the quality of evidence raised on either side of an issue. We would encourage formally debating the points, either as a whole class or in small groups, following a predetermined structure. This has the advantage of diluting emotional standpoints that can get in the way of reasoned scientific discussion.

In meeting the second aim, we describe processes that go on behind the scenes among scientists to ensure that published work in science is as reliable as possible. We suggest a set of scientific ethics, and discuss these as principles guiding the way scientists work, placing them in the wider context of ethical principles that we take for granted in society.

The third aim touches on the darker aspects of doing science – fraudulent behaviour and attempts to deceive. This area of science tends to be hidden. Students need to learn that consequences arise from bad behaviour. Here we focus on scientists who are known to have behaved fraudulently. We suggest how to follow this up in discussion with students.

The ethics of science can be a touchy and sensitive subject. There is a case for saying that too much is expected of teenagers – they may lack the emotional reserves to handle ethical issues appropriately. We leave this for teachers to judge with their students. From a teaching point of view, clearly, handling a range of views held strongly by a group of young people does require a certain skill – we hope that the activities provide a sensible structure and format for helping colleagues with this task.

6.2 Argumentation activities

We suggest two ways of presenting ethical information to students. Both use argumentation techniques – encouraging students to construct logical arguments based on evidence. We describe argumentation tasks in general, then give information about the two approaches.

Time required: About 60 mins
NC Link: 4a, b, c

Learning outcomes

♦ To give students the opportunity to participate in a decision-making process.
♦ To allow students to assess how science influences society positively and negatively.
♦ To consider both sides of an ethical issue.
♦ To consider scientists' responsibility to conduct their research with concern for society.

♦ *General information about argumentation tasks*

Argumentation tasks permit students to develop their ability to understand issues from different perspectives, as well as to analyse and make sense of evidence. Argument in this sense does not mean confrontation, but making a claim and relating this to data, using a warrant. For example:

♦ I am a British citizen (claim)
♦ I was born in London (data)
♦ people who are born in London are automatically British citizens (warrant).

Students can quite easily make claims and give data, but they need to be able to make the connection between them. This is an important skill in science, as evidence is used to draw conclusions. This is not all: there are other types of statement that a good argument may need. We continue the example above to illustrate these:

- this is the legal position (backing)
- this does not apply if your parents are not British (rebuttal)
- you may have a point – but if your parents are from EU countries, it does not matter (qualifier).

These statements allow the argument to be raised to a more sophisticated level, indicating points of contention (rebuttal), use of qualifying statements, and support from different areas providing backing.

This structure illustrates how students can be encouraged to handle scientific information. For a more complete discussion and training sessions for teachers, see Osborne *et al.* (2004).

◆ *Whole-class debate*

Any of the dilemmas in section 6.3 can be adapted for a whole-class debate format. Perhaps surprisingly, many students respond positively to debates. Giving students genuine responsibility tends to bring out positive qualities, and the defined structure provides a controlled atmosphere that they tend to respect. The option exists of inviting guests to be judges (school governors, senior colleagues, or a special community visitor) to lend an edge to the atmosphere. Older students from years 12–13 also make good, perceptive judges, particularly for year 7–8 groups. Filming the event for posterity can add yet another dimension.

To prepare, rephrase the dilemma as a motion likely to provoke debate in your audience. For example, rephrasing the first dilemma (nuclear fission) to 'This house believes scientific research should be used only to benefit society' allows discussion (among other points) as to what 'benefit society' may mean, allowing nuclear fission to be debated from different standpoints. The more obviously provoking 'This house believes in banning nuclear weapons' is likely to stimulate a major row, probably divided on old-fashioned political lines.

Running a debate

- Decide on two teams (normally two students in each), one team in favour and the other against the motion. The students must be capable of delivering a clearly argued speech on their own for about 5 minutes.
- The arguments can be studied by the audience in a preparation lesson. Using the argumentation strategy

suggested (page 118) in a whole-class lesson beforehand may help everyone to identify occasions when evidence is used well. In the debate itself, those not in the teams will vote on the motion and ask questions.

♦ Decide who should be Chair. A strong-minded, popular, authoritative student is usually best, but another colleague could take this role. As class teacher, maintaining an overview rather than becoming involved is advised.

Advice on running a debate is available from the following sources.

♦ The Debating Matters competition (Institute of Ideas; www.debatingmatters.com) provides an opportunity to debate with other schools. The 2007 grand final debate was 'Human genetic engineering is a step too far?'.

♦ The English Speaking Union runs the London Debate Challenge (www.londondebatechallenge.org).

The following text on how to run a debate is drawn from both sources.

The people

♦ Organise two teams – one in favour of the motion and the other against. Have two students in each team.

♦ Organise a Chair to keep time and control. This needs to be someone with authority who will set a good tone for the proceedings. It is good if this can be a student.

♦ The audience must listen to the arguments. Once the arguments have been presented, they may question the teams. Finally, they will vote on the motion.

♦ The Debating Matters competition format has judges – colleagues, visitors or older students – to decide which team presented its arguments best. Judges will give feedback and ask questions.

The room

If this is set up as a special occasion in an unfamiliar room, some basic checks are worthwhile:

♦ arrangement of furniture – see the *Debating Matters Competition Handbook* (Academy of Ideas, 2006) for a good layout

♦ sound or other audiovisual equipment working

- a lectern or similar may be useful for speakers
- glasses of water available for speakers, Chair and judges
- a small bell or gavel available for the Chair to signal ends of speeches, and to get attention
- a clock, visible so speeches can be timed accurately.

The format
The Debating Matters competition format allows 70 minutes for the full debate. Suggested timings are as follows.

Action	Time (minutes)
Introduction of teams and (if using) judges by the Chair	5
Presentations by teams, 5 minutes each person, alternating and starting with the first student *for* the motion	20
Judges' questions (optional) – each judge can ask one question of each team, aiming to push their arguments further and reveal how good their preparation has been	15
Team questions – each team can ask questions of the other team, to probe weaknesses in their arguments	15
Audience questions – the Chair will invite members of the audience to ask questions of the teams, trying to maintain a balance between the two	10
Vote and judges' decision – the Chair invites the audience to vote: those in favour and those against. A tally is made and the final result announced: 'The motion ... is carried' or 'The motion ... is defeated'. The judges announce which team they think actually won the debate, regardless of the audience vote.	5

A short debriefing is a good idea, reminding students not to carry on arguments outside the classroom, telling the teams and Chair they are no longer in these roles, and thanking the judges for their time and opinions. If this is a special occasion, a prize for the winning team is always good.

◆ *Small group discussion activities*

Argumentation tasks can be run on a smaller scale by adapting the material to a different format. Here is a suggested approach to running a debate lesson through small groups.

Time required: about an hour
NC link: 4a, b, c

Starter questions

To promote discussion, the following could be good starters.

◆ The chair/stool on which you sit is/is not mostly empty space.
◆ Man-made carbon dioxide is/is not mainly responsible for global climate change.
◆ If we did not use fertilisers, more people would be starving.

Alternatively, pick non-scientific topics such as the following.

◆ Valentine's Day should be abandoned.
◆ The ban on smoking in public places (imposed in the UK on 1 July 2007) is wrong.
◆ Sport brings out the best in people.

These are all deliberately provocative – in several of the phrases, almost every word could be argued over. Their purpose is to stimulate debate, so assessing ambiguity is part of the point of the exercise.

What to do

◆ Read the claim–data–warrant connection above (page 114). Encourage students to get used to linking claims to evidence, rather than just making random remarks.
◆ Discuss the points for and against one or two of these statements for about 5 minutes each, encouraging students to give evidence for their views.
◆ Establish rules as to how discussions should be conducted, together with the need for evidence to back up points.

Main activity

Select one of the dilemmas from section 6.3 (or a similar topic) for discussion. To encourage students to construct an argument, follow these steps.

◆ Decide on the topic for discussion.
◆ Divide the class into groups of about four students.

♦ Indicate to each group that they must come to a conclusion, either for or against the discussion point.
♦ Introduce prompt questions to show how the information should be organised – suggestions (Osborne *et al.*, 2001) might include:
  – why do you think that?
  – what is your reason for that?
  – can you think of another argument for your view?
  – can you think of an argument against your view?
  – how do you know?
  – what is your evidence?
  – is there another argument for what you believe?
♦ Allow time to collect material to investigate, decide on a viewpoint and organise evidence to support their case. The questions suggested with each dilemma can be used as starting points. A minimum of 30 minutes is advised to allow time to get into the task. This would work well with internet access.

Plenary discussion and review

Groups can present their views in turn, or selected groups may be invited to do so. Using PowerPoint would help address key skills development. Alternatively, the question prompts could be used as a writing frame to structure a poster or exercise book work.
   In a plenary discussion:

♦ try to ensure students see both sides of the dilemma – it may be that a class becomes polarised in one direction
♦ encourage students to weigh up the quality of evidence on either side
♦ draw out arguments both in favour and against.

6.3 Ethical dilemmas

In this section we discuss some familiar scientific topics that raise ethical issues for debate. Each offers the potential for further research and is accompanied by questions. We have given each a provocative title, but feel free to change this to suit the context.

♦ *The development of nuclear weapons – when physics lost its innocence*

The information provided on the CD summarises the science behind the development of nuclear weapons. Einstein's 1939 letter to President Roosevelt is included.

The dilemma

♦ Should scientists stop their research when they find the results could be used for making weapons or other 'bad' uses?
♦ How should scientists control the uses made from their discoveries?
♦ What positive uses have resulted from nuclear fission research?

Further questions

♦ What were the scientists Fermi, Meitner and others trying to do when they started their research into radioactivity? Did they intend to make a nuclear weapon?
♦ Why did Einstein and others write to President Roosevelt?
♦ What effect did the letter have? Do you think this was the effect Einstein wanted?
♦ Some say using the bombs was justified because this ended a war that would have carried on with even greater loss of life. What is your opinion?

♦ *Using animals in experiments – their lives or ours?*

The issue of using animals in experiments has been discussed for years. The arguments and counter-arguments raised about this are presented in a table on the CD for students to analyse. These represent the range of opinion, and students need to decide if the points are good or weak. Background information tries to set out the case for both sides.

The dilemma

Professor Colin Blakemore claims, 'To be consistent in your moral position is difficult. It would involve refusing any form of conventional medical treatment, refusing any drug, carrying a card saying, "Don't help me with conventional medicine because I object to it being tested on animals".'

Should we ban animal testing completely, slowing the progress of medical developments that could benefit humans? To what extent should animal life be regarded as equal to human life?

Further questions

♦ What are the benefits of using animals in experiments?
♦ What do you think of the views expressed in the table? Are these good arguments?

- Why can't the use of animals in experiments be stopped completely?
- In what ways do scientists follow, and not follow, ethical principles in using animals?
- Is it right to target and attack scientists for using animals in experiments?
- If you had a desperately ill child and a new drug was available for their treatment, would you:
  - agree to the treatment only if it hadn't been tested on animals?
  - agree to the treatment regardless of how it had been tested?

◆ *Using human embryos – research at the beginning of humanity*

This is a relatively new dilemma brought about by developments in tissue culture and other areas that have enabled scientists to create conditions to sustain human embryos *in vitro*. The topic touches on the issue of whether using human tissue in this way is morally permissible. One speculative point that could be made is that medicine may have gone through a similar discussion in the sixteenth century, when dissection of human bodies was becoming commonplace. Before this time, information about humans had to be discerned from animal dissection (see Chapter 2). Are we instinctively naturally sensitive about new ways of using human bodies? Background information is provided on the CD.

The dilemma

Should scientists be allowed to use human embryos to develop potentially effective treatments for incurable diseases that many of us may suffer from in later life? Or is human genetic engineering a step too far?

Further questions

- What is the strongest argument in favour of using human embryos in research?
- Why do opponents say using human embryos is not acceptable?
- Very few scientists in the UK have been given licences to experiment on human embryos. Why do we regulate this work so carefully?
- What ethical principles should be agreed on for using human embryos in research?

- If there was an inherited disease in your family, and you knew that embryonic stem cells could be used to develop an effective treatment, would this justify using human embryos in your view?

◆ *The development of genetically modified foods – the latest style of lunch*

Genetically modifying crops to obtain the most produce from an area of land has been practised in what could be described as a natural way for centuries. The technology now exists to use genetic engineering to speed up this process, hence the development of genetically modified (GM) organisms (GMOs). This dilemma tries to set out the scientific arguments surrounding the development of GM food crops and their potential for reducing hunger. Background information is provided on the CD.

The dilemma

Should GM foods be developed, knowing that they will improve the quality of life for millions, but also not knowing what their long-term impact will be?

Further questions

- Would you eat your favourite food if you knew it included ingredients from a GM plant or animal?
- Would you change your answer to the previous question if you had not eaten that favourite food for a year?
- Is it better to keep using fertilisers and other chemicals, or to develop GM crops and animals that don't need them?
- What ethics should control how GM foods are developed and used around the world?
- Should we develop GM foods and just sell and eat them like any other food? Should they be labelled as 'genetically modified'?

6.4 Background information

In this section we discuss how ethics has influenced the practice of science. This topic is not often discussed, probably for reasons such as lack of time, lack of material, and concerns about possible legal issues. In writing this book we have taken care not to use information that could be subject to a legal case – hoping nevertheless that what we provide makes a start on a topic that is certainly part of how science works.

◆ *What are 'scientific ethics'?*

Generally, ethics offer a guide to conduct or a statement of moral value that distinguishes between acceptable and unacceptable behaviour. If we stop to think about it, almost all aspects of our lives are regulated by ethics. Social ethics are ingrained in us as we grow up: learning when to say 'please', 'thank you', 'excuse me' and 'sorry' are simple examples. Professions, hobbies and interests all have ethics embodied in them. Teachers' professional behaviour is regulated by the General Teaching Council; that of doctors and lawyers by the General Medical Council and the Law Society, respectively. Sports have ethical codes that prohibit cheating and being rude to officials, and promote playing by the rules. Religions have sets of ethics to which believers subscribe: these include the Ten Commandments in Judaism/Christianity; the five principles of Buddhism; the principle of honesty emphasised by Confucius; and the emphasis on working towards reincarnation in Hinduism. Some scientists choose to take membership of UK-based professional organisations such as the Royal Society of Chemistry, the Institute of Physics and the Institute of Biology, and their equivalents worldwide. These have ethical standards, which their members abide by.

Whether scientists are members of a professional organisation or not, their work is governed by ethics, reflecting the goal of science – the pursuit of truthful, new knowledge and understanding about the physical and natural world. These ethics are not formally written down and may vary according to circumstance. A majority of scientists would probably agree with these fairly obvious statements:

- ◆ be honest – don't publish fraudulent data; don't make up, trim down, smooth out or misrepresent data
- ◆ be careful – avoid careless errors and any sloppiness in all aspects of scientific work
- ◆ be open – share data, results, methods, equipment and theories, and be open to criticism by showing findings to others
- ◆ be responsible – where humans could be genuinely affected by the findings of an experiment, use the media to publicise results widely
- ◆ don't plagiarise – give credit for the work of others
- ◆ enjoy intellectual freedom – feel free to pursue research in areas of interest and to criticise old ideas.

All these are important, but being honest is perhaps the most important. Without honesty, the truth cannot be established. Science would then become subject to unreliable lies. Human error may occur, but scientists' ways of working should ensure this is minimised.

We can discuss reasons for some of the other statements, too. Being open about scientific discoveries, rather than keeping them hidden, broadens access to knowledge, helping to speed up the acquisition of new ideas. Being criticised ensures that new knowledge and ideas are tested by others, helping to make scientific discoveries reliable. Although scientists generally tend to avoid the media, there is a responsibility to ensure the public hear about findings that could have a significant impact on society. Crediting the work of others helps preserve an atmosphere within which data, ideas and experimental methods can be shared freely between colleagues. Having the freedom to investigate according to interest means that science is free from political control, so scientists are not working to fulfil sinister goals set by dictators, or simply to make a profit.

Other ethical statements about how scientists work apply equally to everyone. For example, working within national laws, such as those respecting health and safety and employment; acting with integrity; showing colleagues respect and not discriminating between colleagues on ethnic, racial or gender grounds.

◆ *Why do we need scientific ethics?*

This may be an obvious question, but one way of answering it is to consider what would happen if we did not have scientific ethics. If this is discussed with students, allow some thinking time and then find out their views. 'Anarchy' probably sums up what these might be. The pursuit of 'truth' relies on the idea of doing this in a truthful and honest way – if there are no standards for obtaining that knowledge, can it really be relied on as the truth? We are touching on philosophy here, and for the sake of keeping things clear and simple, we suggest some points to draw out in discussion. In general, ethics provide scientists with an in-built code of behaviour that is self-policed. We will look at these internal policing systems and their effectiveness later (page 131). Meanwhile, the following are reasons to support the ethical code for science.

♦ We rely on scientific information being produced in an honest and true way, being a true account of events or the most truthful explanation possible. Without this, science will not be believed or accepted as true knowledge.

♦ Science is often regarded as the ultimate search for truth, and this standard cannot be maintained without applying an ethical code.

♦ Research often involves collaboration – ethics provide a code for collaboration among people from widely different cultures and backgrounds.

♦ Science is accountable to the public – often public money is spent on research, and it is important that this is spent in an honest way.

♦ Science is perceived as reliable and worth supporting – if science had a reputation for being carried out by liars and cheats, then non-scientists would rightly question any discovery that was made.

♦ Science also impinges on social morals – for example, using animals and humans in testing. Scientific ethics ensure codes of practice are in place to minimise potential harm and that science practice complies with health and safety and other laws.

Ethics provide a moral structure or code for how scientists should conduct themselves. Severe penalties arise when ethics are ignored – scientists found to be frauds, or who are particularly difficult to work with, risk their reputation and ultimately losing their career.

♦ *Who cheats at science?*

Why do they cheat? And how do they do it? We can safely assume that the vast majority of science is carried out in accordance with ethical principles. One discussion to have with students is the extent to which *they* cheat – how easy is it? How tempting is it? What stops them? What motivates them?

There are three main reasons why scientists cheat: career pressure; believing they know the answer; and simply knowing they can get away with it.

Career pressure

Scientists work under pressure, like anyone else, and may be tempted to bend the rules. Being a good research scientist requires publications, successful grant applications and achieving results. Prizes, awards and high status beckon for the best. When jobs, career prospects, a new laboratory and promotions are on the line, or the prospect looms of a competitor being first to make the big discovery, the temptation to fabricate and deceive can be high. More practically, research scientists often work on short-term contracts. Getting more work relies on achieving more funding, which relies on getting results. Where is the line drawn between keeping a job and being 100% honest?

The temptation to cheat is there for everyone, even (or perhaps particularly) for well known scientists attracted by big research grants and making discoveries that bring fame. A well-documented case in recent years is that of Hwang Woo-suk, the South Korean stem cell researcher who in 2006 was found to have made fraudulent claims about the progress of his research, and was disgraced (Box 6.1). The potential of stem cell research for treating many common diseases emphasises the scandal.

Hwang Woo-suk's case is extreme. The potential rewards for success in stem cell research are great – everyone wants the perfect cure for diseases, with no side-effects and excellent results. Nationally, Hwang was a hero, treated like the scientific equivalent of a rock star. He had enormous funding for research, commanded the work of many people and was acclaimed worldwide. Hwang seems genuinely to have believed his theories about cloning human stem cells. His mistake was to claim proof too early. This perhaps helps to explain why he did not regard repeating his techniques and results as important – he was too absorbed, carried away by possibilities.

Box 6.1 Hwang Woo-suk, an example of serious scientific fraud

Who is Hwang Woo-suk?
Hwang Woo-suk is a South Korean research scientist. He was born in 1953, during the Korean War. His father died when he was only 5 years old, and he had a poor upbringing. Hwang trained as a vet, then carried out research in animal reproduction, a science called theriogenology. Hwang built a research career in cloning, using genetics to make identical copies of organisms.

What did he do?
In 1999 he claimed to have cloned a cow, and in 2002 a pig. In 2004 he shot to fame, claiming the 'holy grail' – cloning human embryos and taking stem cells from one of them. In

---

2005 he topped this, claiming development of 11 personalised stem cell lines. These results were published in the American journal *Science* and hailed as great achievements – human cells are difficult to clone and personalised stem cells are regarded as the dream for medical developments.

Why was his claim so special?
Having a stock of personalised stem cells means treatments can be designed individually. Stem cells contain the information necessary to become many types of cell. Theoretically, new liver cells, nerves or muscle could be grown from your own stem cells. If his results were true, the potential was huge for medical advances in treating illnesses such as Parkinson's disease, diabetes and heart disease, as individual treatments could be offered. So far, only drug treatments or organ donations are possible. These involve bad side-effects and/or extra drugs to stop us rejecting 'foreign' cells.

What was his fraud?
He lied about the human cloning and stem cell experiments. The results were fabricated.

How was the fraud found out?
To make the human embryos and stem cells, eggs are needed. Hwang was accused of obtaining these from his own female employees, which is against the law – only volunteer eggs can be used. This started an investigation, which showed that the human stem cells did not have the same DNA as the patients he claimed they came from. They were not personalised. The human embryo clone claim was also false.

What happened next?
Hwang resigned from his post at Seoul National University in January 2006. He claimed the results had been sabotaged. In May 2006 he was arrested on fraud and embezzlement charges. He was accused of using Korean government money to buy a car, paying politicians to back his research and women to give him their eggs. This is the up-to-date position at the time of writing.

Believing they know the answer

Scientists can become so caught up in their theories that they may believe they are true before experimental data support their claim. One step further leads them to make unrealistic claims in research publications. Hwang's case showed elements of this. The likelihood is that what he claimed *will be* true, but in a few years time, when more experiments have been done.

A similar situation faced Jan Hendrik Schön, a talented young researcher working in nanotechnology at a German university, supported financially by Bell Labs, an American technology company. He wrote a large number of papers in a short period, publishing data that supported complex electronic theories. The sheer number of publications and significance of the claims made caused suspicion. Someone spotted that the 'noise' on two of his graphs in two different papers looked identical. Eventually, the case unravelled. Schön admitted that he had fabricated some data, and had perhaps used the same data on more than one occasion by accident. He had worked alone and had not kept any records of his experiments. He had no data stored on his computer, and no artefacts from any experiments. After an investigation, Schön lost his job, being found guilty of 16 counts of misconduct. Part of Schön's defence was that he believed his claims would be found to be true in time.

Knowing they can get away with it

Cheating on results is easy. Even one of the authors of this book admits to faking the results of a school genetics experiment using *Drosophila* (fruit flies) in the 1970s. We mated flies with two different eye colours, one carried a dominant gene (properly called an allele), the other being recessive. After 2 weeks, we had the generation of flies that would demonstrate Mendel's law of inheritance, showing the dominant and recessive eye colours in a 3:1 ratio. To do the count, we had to anaesthetise the flies, using ether-soaked cotton wool plugs. Flies escaped while we swapped the test-tube stoppers for the anaesthetic-soaked ones. Wary of killing them, we tipped the flies out before they were fully asleep. More flew away. The results were the exact opposite of those predicted – the rest were flying around the lab. We risked a bad mark by reporting the truth, or, by switching the figures, could claim a perfect result and get an excellent mark, knowing our busy teacher would not check. We cheated and took the grade A. Whether we could have got the same grade by saying honestly that our results had flown away will never be known.

One reason why scientists cheat is because they know they can get away with it. Although results are supposed to be reliable, in that someone *could* replicate them, this is rarely put to the test. In the case of my school experiment, we were expecting a 3:1 ratio, so all I did was to confirm this. Scientists publishing results in journals may well smooth out experimental noise, remove the oddest result, or flatten the curved part of a straight-line graph to emphasise a point. This does not always detract from the overall result, or the impact of the work. Table 6.1 (page 130) indicates that some well known scientists may have been guilty of this, but have still retained their reputation.

There are a few extreme cases of scientists who have built their career on fabricating results. The journalists Broad and Wade (1982) cite the example of Elias Alsabti, who operated on the edge of the American scientific research scene for a number of years. Alsabti is said to have passed off the work of others as his own, an offence called plagiarism. His critics accused him of finding work in obscure journals, reworking it slightly and then republishing it in more prestigious journals to build his reputation. The USA is such a large country that even though colleagues became suspicious, Alsabti could leave a post and obtain another one without difficulty. Eventually, the suspicions became too great and he was forced to leave science. Alsabti pursued his career more-or-less unchecked for some years, effectively trading on weaknesses in the publications system, and the way in which people generally take others at face value.

Examples of scientific fraud

Table 6.1 lists examples of scientific fraud. We have been cautious, including only the best-documented cases that are not, as far as we are aware, subject to ongoing legal wrangling. There are different types of fraud, for example:

- claiming a bigger role in a major discovery than is really true
- not following established scientific practice or procedures in setting up experiments
- stretching points in arguments beyond what is reasonable to support a personal viewpoint or hypothesis
- putting the same results or calculations in many papers with a different twist, to achieve more publications
- using someone else's results without acknowledgement – plagiarism
- committing a hoax, fabricating results then claiming a 'discovery', for example by calculating results rather than reporting experimental results, or by putting artefacts in the ground and then digging them up.

Table 6.1 *Examples of scientific fraud*

Scientist, lifespan, area of science	Fraud topic	Date	Details
Gregor Mendel, 1822–84, genetics	Selecting data to prove laws of inheritance	1860s	Mendel's data are thought by some scientists to have been too accurate to be true! He may have been selective in his reporting
Robert Millikan, 1868–1953, physics	Selecting data for the oil-drop experiment	1909	Data from the experiment were used to calculate the charge on an electron. Millikan carefully selected results that fitted with his theory, instead of reporting all data
Charles Dawson, 1864–1916, archaeology/ anthropology	Creating 'Piltdown Man' from ape and human bones	1912	A jawbone of an orang utan was passed off as that of an early human. This 'find' helped explain human evolution. The fraud was discovered in the 1920s, but Piltdown Man was finally disregarded as a forgery only in 1953
Stanley Pons, 1943– and Martin Fleischmann, 1927 –, physics	Claiming cold fusion	1989	The pair showed how to generate excess heat from nuclear reactions at close to room temperature and pressure. They were accused of sloppy work and inaccurate results, but they claim the effect is real
Jan Hendrik Schön, 1970–, physics	Fabricating nanotechnology data	2001	Schön re-used data in several papers and did mathematical calculations to produce data for others, rather than doing experiments. He admitted falsifying data, but also claimed some errors were genuine mistakes. He lost his job and was banned from doing funded research in Germany, where the work took place

Examples of most of these can be researched quite easily – try entering 'scientific fraud' in an internet search engine. The extent to which frauds happen by accident, or are carried out deliberately to create a false impression, can be discussed. Also, variations in seriousness between different examples can be considered – what constitutes a serious breach of scientists' ethics?

We can assume that most scientists are humble, honest, hard-working people seeking truth in their area of expertise. Where issues arise, they may be subject to subtle reasons for not following ethical practice. For example, results may not show what was expected, possibly putting the financial backer of the research in a bad light. In these cases, results may be suppressed or played down. For example, two companies (or research groups) compete for a discovery, knowing that large profits (or acclaim) are available to the winner. One gets results that put making the discovery on hold. They suppress publication, as the competitor could gain an advantage both from knowing their rival had difficulties, and from the reasons for those difficulties. It could be asked whether this is cheating – or simply good business practice? What is the role of the individual scientist in the decision to keep the results quiet? Should a scientist 'blow the whistle', admitting failures, even if this potentially bankrupts his/her company or damages the research group's prestige?

◆ *How does science prevent cheating?*

A three-way system of internal policing operates worldwide to attempt to prevent cheating in science. The three methods are:

- ◆ peer review
- ◆ the referee system
- ◆ replication.

These work in slightly different ways depending on the field of science, so a reader with a background in a different science may (rightly) disagree with some of the details. For example, the first two terms are used interchangeably to describe the processes of assessing grant applications and the quality of research papers for publication. We report from our experience as scientists and academics.

Peer review and the referee system

Research grant applications are assessed by experts, called peer reviewers or referees, to determine if scientists are planning to make good use of money. Research funds often come from public donations – Cancer Research UK is the largest donor-funded charity in the world – or from taxpayers through government departments and research councils. For big projects involving large sums of money, a peer-review/referee team representing the financier keeps oversight of the work. This may be called a steering group. Their role is to ensure target dates are met, money is not diverted out of the project, expert staff are employed, and appropriate methods are used. Researchers submit reports at various stages. The final report is often graded by the funding agency on the basis of the value of the results – obtaining further backing can depend on the grade awarded.

Similar projects may be funded for several different research groups simultaneously. This ensures collaboration, as well as providing extra security in getting results should one group fail or experience difficulties. The possibility of error is also reduced by collaborative working. Some very large projects (such as the human genome project, space exploration and building particle colliders) are so expensive that collaboration between countries is the only way to fund them. In these cases, international supervisory panels are set up.

Publications

Scientists publish their work in specialist journals. This ensures that results are subject to scrutiny and methods and data are shared in the community. A scientist who wants to report findings will write a paper for publication. Some or all members of a research group may be listed as authors. The paper is sent to the journal's editor, who sends it on to experts in that area of work. They act as referees or peer reviewers. Each reviewer reads the paper independently of the others and sends comments back to the editor, who compares the comments and makes a decision about publication. The paper can be rejected, sent back for further work or accepted.

Replication

Scientists have to report in a way that enables others to repeat their findings. In principle, results must have the potential to be replicated. In practice, this is rarely done due to time and financial constraints, and variations in local conditions, such as unavailability of equipment and/or staff. Scientists may have to compromise money, time, their own ideas and those of the funding agency in achieving results. They rarely have the luxury of doing as many tests as they would like.

No mechanism is perfect – for example, the papers for which Hwang and Schön had fabricated data were peer-reviewed and accepted. Some fraudsters succeed, at least for a limited period, because no-one attempted to repeat reported experiments. Using calculated data rather than experimental data can go unnoticed until someone really takes time to check. Students can research how scientists' frauds have been revealed.

Although the policing systems are not perfect, no-one has yet come up with anything better. The occasions on which scientists have behaved deliberately fraudulently are almost certainly very few, for all the reasons discussed above. If mistakes are made, these are most likely due to human error. For practical purposes, ensuring all results are replicated before publication is impossible, given the number of experiments, papers and journals involved. Non-scientists could not be involved in policing science, as they would not have the depth of knowledge required for successful detection of faults and fraud. We have to live with science as it is – largely free from external critique and policing, but with weaknesses within.

6.5 Summary

We have tried to highlight that scientific discoveries can have disadvantages as well as advantages. These can bring dilemmas that are difficult to resolve, raising ethical questions for society. Students can address these using argumentation strategies, focusing on scientific evidence and using this to support claims.

This chapter also illustrates occasions when scientists overstep the ethical bounds that govern their practice. Sometimes this is out of over-enthusiasm for, and anticipation of, their discoveries – even so, scientists whose professional behaviour is questioned generally find it difficult to sustain their careers.

The role of ethics in how science works needs to be shown to students as the 'warts-and-all' side of the scientific coin.

6.6 References and resources

General, argumentation and debating

Academy of Ideas (2006) *Institute of Ideas & Pfizer Debating Matters Competition Handbook*. Debating Matters, London. www.debatingmatters.com/module_images/Debating%20Matters%20Competition%20Handbook.pdf

Broad, W. and Wade, N. (1982) *Betrayers of the Truth*. Oxford: Oxford University Press.

Osborne, J., Erduran, S., Simon, S. and Monk, M. (2001) Enhancing the quality of argument in school science. *School Science Review* 82: 63–70.

Osborne, J., Erduran, S. and Simon, S. (2004) *Ideas, Evidence and Argument in Science. CPD Training Pack*. London: King's College.

Argumentation resources are available from: www.kcl.ac.uk/schools/sspp/education/research/projects/ideas.html

Debating Matters: www.debatingmatters.com

London Debate Challenge: www.londondebatechallenge.org

The development of nuclear weapons

The Nobel Foundation account is as reliable as any:
http://nobelprize.org/educational_games/peace/nuclear_weapons/readmore.html

This website is a thorough archive: http://nuclearweaponarchive.org

A historical approach with many excellent photographs is presented through the USA's National Atomic Museum: www.atomicmuseum.com/tour/manhattanproject.cfm

Spartacus schoolnet provides access to documents used at the time, including letters from scientists to the US President and evidence of UK/US collaboration: www.spartacus.schoolnet.co.uk/USAmanhattan.htm

Atomic Archive: www.atomicarchive.com/Docs/ManhattanProject/index.shtml

Animal experimentation

Using animal experiments in research is a 'hot topic' on the BBC website: www.bbc.co.uk/science/hottopics/animalexperiments/alternatives.shtml

The Dr Hadwen Trust claims to be the UK's largest charity funding non-animal experimentation research: www.drhadwentrust.org

The Wellcome Trust website has information on using animals in research, but this is a bit more technical: www.wellcome.ac.uk/doc_WTD002764.html

Huntingdon Life Sciences: www.huntingdon.com

Stem cell research

The Association of Medical Research Charities offers a compilation of information on stem cell research: www.amrc.org.uk

A recent news report setting out the case for using human embryos: http://news.bbc.co.uk/1/hi/health/6760707.stm

The case for using adult stem cells is discussed at: www.21stcenturysciencetech.com/articles/winter01/stem_cell.html

A religious standpoint on this topic can be found at: www.religioustolerance.org/emb_rese.htm

A technical account is given at: http://aappolicy.aappublications.org/cgi/content/full/pediatrics;108/3/813

Human Fertilisation and Embryology Authority: www.hfea.gov.uk

This *Daily Telegraph* article reviews the latest developments in permitting human embryo research: www.telegraph.co.uk/news/main.jhtml?xml=/news/2007/09/06/nhybrid106.xml

GM foods

Reasoned debate about GMOs can be found here: www.ornl.gov/sci/techresources/Human_Genome/elsi/gmfood.shtml

A wide range of articles on this topic are available through the New Scientist website: www.newscientist.com/channel/life/gm-food

The Children's BBC (CBBC) website has information in a very simple format: http://news.bbc.co.uk/cbbcnews/hi/find_out/guides/tech/gm_foods/newsid_1746000/1746923.stm

An article on world hunger is available at: http://news.ninemsn.com.au/article.aspx?id=157083

Scientific ethics

A good general article about scientific ethics by David Resnik can be found at: www.physics.emich.edu/mthomsen/resn1.htm

The US National Institute of Environmental Health Sciences has a very good timeline for research ethics: www.niehs.nih.gov/research/resources/bioethics/timeline.cfm

Hwang Woo-suk is discussed at: http://news.bbc.co.uk/1/hi/world/asia-pacific/4554704.stm
www.theregister.co.uk/2006/01/12/hwang_apology

Jan Hendrik Schön's case is described at: http://physicsworld.com/cws/article/print/11352

7 *Error, risk and hazard*

7.1 Why do you need this chapter?

The aims of this chapter are to:

♦ examine occasions when science makes mistakes
♦ establish the difference between risk and hazard
♦ suggest ways of helping students understand how to estimate risk.

The image of the 'mad scientist' is potent – even young children, when asked to draw a scientist, will probably make an image of a (usually) male person with spiky hair, wearing glasses and a coat, engaged in a dangerous activity, exploding chemicals or weapons. They are exaggerating cartoon images – but the message is clear, that science is dangerous, risky, and to do it you need to be crazy.

In this chapter we try to redress the balance. We point out that, occasionally, science does make mistakes. Although it is not an excuse, the vast majority of scientists don't intend to make mistakes through their work, but rather seek truthful knowledge that can benefit society. But despite their best efforts, things can go wrong. This is part of how science works – in school we almost always teach the end results of often-painstaking scientific effort that resulted in 'correct' knowledge, without ever regarding experiments that failed, mistakes or errors.

The image of science as 'dangerous' also needs to be addressed. Students need to understand the difference between risk and hazard, and to be able to analyse risk appropriately. We offer activities that emphasise this through role play and case studies.

The background information provides supporting material for the activities. We address reasons for teaching risk and hazard effectively, with a brief assessment of the benefits this could bring.

7.2 Activities

◆ *Personal choice, personal risk*

This is adapted from an activity in the *AS Science for Public Understanding* course (Melamed, 2005).

Learning outcomes

- ◆ To assess the varying degrees of risk associated with activities.
- ◆ To realise that we are often irrational in our estimation of personal risk.

Time required: about 20 minutes
NC link: 4a

This task involves asking students to complete a personal risk-analysis sheet listing ten different activities, provided on the CD. Working in groups, the class can then discuss their attitudes to the risks associated with each, deciding on the five most risky and the five least risky activities. They are asked to come up with reasons for their choices.

Plenary discussion

The following points may be drawn out as factors known to affect our analysis of personal risk.

- ◆ Using limited information – media reports are often accepted as providing reliable information, when in fact data may be reported in a skewed way to create a particular impression.
- ◆ Media reports can give the impression that activities are much more risky than they really are – newspapers sell more if they can report a disaster. This can create the impression that the activity behind an event must in itself be dangerous, when in fact the event is extremely rare.
- ◆ Not knowing the full extent of the risk – this is another example of using limited information. We may simply be ignorant, making estimates without searching out further details that can help make a more accurate assessment.
- ◆ Personal experience and habit lead us to underestimate risks involved in our everyday activities. For example, we may use cars every day, but not think about being involved in an accident, even though accidents are relatively common.
- ◆ We are also very adept at twisting risk so it does not appear to apply to us – for example, 'I can smoke and not get cancer' or 'I am a good driver so I will not crash'.

♦ We are less likely to accept imposed risks than voluntary ones. For example, we can protest about a mobile telephone mast or a nuclear power station being sited nearby as risks to our health, yet still smoke heavily. Smoking heavily is likely to pose the bigger risk to health.

Essentially, we are inconsistent when calculating and applying risk to our own lives.

♦ Bad science, good science

This activity is a comprehension exercise based on the thalidomide tragedy. The story illustrates how a scientific error can have disastrous effects. We find out how the USA was spared from a thalidomide disaster by the robust actions of the FDA (Federal Drug Adminstration) medical officer who considered the drug application. The activity overlaps with material in Chapter 6 on ethics and Chapter 4 on evidence.

Learning outcomes
♦ To understand that scientists can make mistakes because they do not know all the facts.
♦ To understand the role of evidence in making correct decisions.
♦ To realise that professional ethics can contribute to averting disaster.

Time required: about 40 minutes
NC link: 4a, 4b, 4c, 1b, 3c

Background information
The thalidomide tragedy is well known. This activity takes a more unusual angle by exploring the tragedy from the perspective of the medical officer responsible for approving the drug for sale in the USA. A task sheet is on the CD.

Thalidomide was developed by a German drug company in the 1950s. The drug was presented as a non-toxic alternative to barbiturates (sleeping tablets), appearing to be non-toxic even when large doses were taken. The drug was also found to help control morning sickness in the first three months of pregnancy. Although drug testing and clinical trials were much less rigorous at that time, some clinical evidence of effectiveness was expected. In the thalidomide case, this was from experiments on mice.

The teratogenic effects of thalidomide (birth defects) went unnoticed until reports showed that women taking the drug were giving birth to deformed children, some of whom died. Initially, these reports were dismissed as inexplicable coincidence. By late 1961, sufficient evidence had been built up that thalidomide was responsible – by then about 10 000 children with defects had been born worldwide, of whom around 5000 did not survive childhood.

Thalidomide was found later to be racemic – this means the molecule can exist in two mirror-image forms, called optical isomers, as each isomer rotates plane-polarised light in opposite directions. Chemists call this property 'handedness' – the atoms in the thalidomide molecule can bond in two different ways that can't be superimposed on each other, although they are the same substance. In the same way, one person can't lay their two hands directly on top of each other, palms upwards, with all fingers matching. The two forms of thalidomide have different effects – one is active, exactly as the drug company claimed. The other causes birth defects. The original drug was a mixture of both forms. The company was unaware of this at the time. Since then, pharmaceutical companies have devised ways of identifying and testing drugs that have optical isomers.

Frances Kelsey was honoured for her judgement, steadfastness and professionalism in her handling of the thalidomide case. She was awarded the President's Award for Distinguished Federal Civilian Service – the equivalent of the George Cross in the UK – by President Kennedy in 1962, and played a major part in establishing strict drug-assessment procedures in the USA. At the time of writing, Frances Kelsey is still alive – in 2000 she was inducted into the USA's National Women's Hall of Fame. In 2005 she finally retired from the FDA, aged 90.

You could discuss drug testing and clinical trials today with students. In March 2006, a group of eight volunteers took a previously untested drug, TGN1412, in a clinical trial. Two were given placebos. The other six developed life-threatening multiple-organ failure. Although all survived, the case shows that even 50 years after thalidomide, with much more thorough testing systems in place, outcomes are not always predictable. Resource materials (see list) give further information about this case.

Answers to questions
1. Difficulty in sleeping and morning sickness in pregnancy.
2. The claims about the positive effects were accurate.
3. No, the drug had not been tested on pregnant women.

4. Answers may vary. Possible answers are:
   a) The drug was not tested thoroughly
   b) It seemed a quick solution to a common problem
   c) The company ignored the problems
5. The USA was a very large market, which meant that the company could expect big profits.
6. Her job was to consider applications from drug companies that wanted to sell their products in the USA.
7. The evidence was not strong enough. She used her past experience to say that more tests were needed. She found side-effects reported in the literature and insisted on these being resolved.
8. Kelsey resisted the pressure and would not give in to bullying.
9. Kelsey relied on hard evidence. She asked questions and used her past experiences. She had tested drugs before, and applied her knowledge to a new situation. She was sceptical.
10. Many more children would have been born with birth defects due to thalidomide. As the USA is a very large country, and the drug had proved popular elsewhere, approving thalidomide for sale could have been a very serious disaster affecting many children and their families.

Plenary discussion

The task sheet on the CD provides space for students to summarise the scientific error that caused the thalidomide tragedy, and the good science that helped avert disaster, at least in the USA. The following points may be drawn out here.

♦ Scientists do sometimes make mistakes – this can be from ignorance, genuine human error, or by doing bad science.
♦ Prior experience is important in learning to do good science.
♦ Taking note of observations and relying on sound evidence is important, even though others may think differently.
♦ The ability to ask questions that can help obtain more data is important.
♦ Being a professional (scientist) means having and keeping high standards in your work, not going against your beliefs by giving way to pressure.

♦ *MMR: what's the risk?*

Confidence in the measles, mumps, rubella (MMR) triple vaccine has declined since 1998. A team of doctors presented information about 12 autistic children with bowel problems, including data about their immunisations. This was misinterpreted by the media as a claim that receiving the MMR vaccination could cause autism, even though the doctors never actually said this at the time. Poor awareness and lack of understanding of the risks associated with having the vaccination and getting measles, mumps or rubella have led to reduced vaccination levels. This activity, seen through the eyes of parents, explores how people analyse risk.

Learning outcomes

◆ To understand that people have different ways of analysing risk.
◆ To assess information to help make more accurate assessments of risk.
◆ To consider accurate information about the MMR vaccine.

Time required: about 30 minutes
NC link: 4a, 4c, 2d

Students are asked to consider four viewpoints of fictional parents, each with a 1-year-old baby who could have the MMR vaccine, using the task sheet on the CD. Two are in favour of vaccination, one is doubtful and the fourth is against. The reasons for their views are based on their different assessments of the risk associated with the vaccine and with getting measles, mumps or rubella, together with any associated complications.

Students read the viewpoints and consider them without any further information. They rank the views and indicate why they have come up with this ranking, based on the parents' analysis of risk.

Next, they read background information cards with facts relating to the MMR vaccine and the diseases. The fact sheet is on the CD. They then reassess their analysis of the parents' views, together with any changes to their ranking.

Plenary discussion

Ask students what arguments they would raise with Dawn and Peter to persuade them to change their minds, or to help them make a decision. Their views can be contrasted with those of Ken and Hayley, who have used risk more wisely in their statements.

Points to draw out:

◆ Variation in people's viewpoints about scientific issues may depend on the way they analyse risk.
◆ Some people (e.g. Dawn) add entirely separate risks together and make erroneous conclusions.

- Others cannot weigh up different risks against each other (e.g. Peter).
- We are all guilty of twisting risks when these apply to ourselves (or our children).
- Emotions can get in the way of making rational decisions.
- In the case of MMR, the vaccination rate has fallen to around 80% in some areas, making a UK measles epidemic possible – vaccination rates of around 95% are needed to ensure immunity in a population.

♦ *Bird flu in Burnham!*

This activity is a role-play based on a fictional scenario of a bird flu outbreak in a small country town. It is written a little tongue-in-cheek, with a mix of characters.

Learning outcomes

- To analyse risk and hazard associated with a possible infection.
- To debate an open-ended situation about an environmental issue.
- To consider the value of evidence in making scientific decisions.

Time required: about an hour
NC links: 4a, 4b, 2d, 3c

Running a role-play can be a good way of learning through stimulating debate. Here the focus is on the difference between risk and hazard, and the management of that risk.

A fictional newspaper report sets the scene – two swans have died from H5N1 infection. This is the virus responsible for avian influenza that has lead to human deaths elsewhere in the world. The virus is a hazard. As the birds have died locally, the risk that local people could be infected is higher than that for people in the wider area. At greatest risk of infection are people who work with poultry, as the virus can cross the species barrier. The council leader has decided to hold an emergency meeting at which views on how to manage the risk will be discussed. She is taking responsibility for ensuring the right advice is taken.

The briefs, available on the CD, are as follows.

- The local vet – she is charged with the task of arguing for restrictions on bird movement, possibly culling wild and farmed birds, restricting movement of poultry, banning any bird fairs, pigeon-racing and other country events, as well as preventing local people using the river. She needs to have evidence for the risk presented to local people.

♦ The local MP – he is not a scientist, but is good at picking up and inferring risk where this should be minimised. He has heard the stories from abroad and wants to make sure the local population is protected. He does not understand the difference between risk and hazard, thinking that everyone is now at great risk of infection.

♦ The chicken farmer – his livelihood depends on his flock of chickens, yet he is most at risk of infection. He wants to find a way to save his poultry, and not get infected himself.

♦ The council leader – she is responsible for managing the risk. She needs to take advice and hear all sides. She will have to put into action any agreed plan, so needs to be able to justify any decision made.

♦ The local environmental campaigner – he does not want to have any restrictions. He thinks the risk of infection is being overstated. Any restrictions could have considerable consequences for the environment.

The strongest opposing roles are those of the vet and the environmental campaigner. The vet will take the most cautious line, opposed by the campaigner who thinks the risks are overestimated. The MP is a 'red herring', playing on ignorance. The chicken farmer is scared, grumpy and ignorant, prepared to claim that he needs to keep his chickens. The council leader has to navigate between the viewpoints and come up with a plan to manage the risk.

The resources listed can be used to research information.

Running the lesson
The role-play does not need to take too long – allow about 20 minutes or so. Before you begin, give students time to research their roles using the resources listed on page 150.

Plenary discussion
Debrief the participants, ensuring they are told they are no longer the vet, council leader, etc. Time could be provided to write a report on the meeting.

Points to draw out:

♦ the focus is on the risks associated with bird flu infection
♦ the virus itself presents a hazard

- the risk is different for different individuals – the chicken farmer, anglers, and others who regularly come into contact with birds are most at risk of infection
- the risk of human-to-human infection is minimal.

Other points to bear in mind include:

- the virus could change to allow human-to-human infection
- as birds are mobile, there is no guarantee that risk management is going to be really successful.

Those not taking on briefs can listen to the arguments and write follow-up newspaper reports.

7.3 Background information

◆ *Scientific errors*

Using incorrect scientific knowledge

Chapter 1 (page 7) describes the 'black box' image of doing science – something is known to be inside the box, but we have to do experiments, collect evidence and propose hypotheses to find out what it might be. Following this process, scientists go through many phases that do not bring success. They may make incorrect decisions, try experiments that yield nothing, or draw conclusions on the basis of evidence that later proves to be wrong. Eventually, knowledge is produced that stands up to further scrutiny and is accepted as accurate. This tells us that great scientific discoveries cannot be delivered to order – they don't come like sofas, picked out in the fabric we choose and brought to the house. We can't 'do' science to our own design, like we might paint a picture or decorate a cake. Neither can we predict when a great discovery might be made – this could take minutes, days, months or years of work. Science is not a 'once-for-all' subject, but represents a steady process of unravelling knowledge. Trails that finally prove to be wrong, deceiving or are blind alleys all contribute to how science works. Occasionally, wrong information is given too much credence, leading to bad decision-making that can have a major impact.

Table 7.1 summarises some well known scientific errors. Most were based on discoveries that were made innocently – scientists were acting in good faith and in the genuine belief that their work constituted good contributions to knowledge and wellbeing.

Table 7.1 Scientific errors, causes, consequences and resolutions

Scientific error	Date	Scientist(s)	Background	What happened next
N-rays (named after the University of Nancy where they were 'seen')	1903	René-Prosper Blondlot	N-rays were proposed to be emitted from most substances, including the human body. No-one could replicate the findings	Robert Wood went to Blondlot's laboratory. He secretly took away essential pieces of equipment. Blondlot and his assistant still claimed to see the rays. Wood claimed they were lying and deceiving themselves
Cold fusion	1989	Martin Fleischmann and Stanley Pons	Reacting two atomic nuclei together at room temperature and pressure and using relatively simple equipment. This was thought to be impossible as the amounts of energy emitted are huge	Fleischmann and Pons were accused of sloppy practice. Replication of their results has proved difficult, although some scientists have claimed success. Scientists cannot agree whether cold fusion is really occurring
Chlorofluorocarbons (CFCs)	1930s	Thomas Midgley	Midgley discovered Freon (dichloro-difluoromethane) for use as a refrigerant. A family of chemicals, CFCs, was invented with properties that made them useful for aerosols, heat pumps, asthma inhalers and fridges	In 1985, Joe Farman and colleagues at the British Antarctic Survey reported significant loss of ozone above Antarctica. At about the same time, Sherry Rowland and Mario Molina published work showing that CFCs reacted with ozone in the atmosphere
DDT (dichlorodi-phenyltrichloro-ethane)	1874, 1939	Paul Hermann Müller	DDT was first made in 1874. Müller noticed its insecticide properties in the 1930s. DDT was used effectively from the Second World War onwards to help stop the spread of insect-borne diseases such as malaria and typhus	American biologist Rachel Carson published *Silent Spring*, claiming that DDT caused cancer in humans and threatened wildlife. There was a big public outcry, leading to DDT being banned in the 1970s and 1980s
Hubble Space Telescope (HST) mirror	1990	Perkin-Elmer, an optical instrument company	The main mirror was imperfect to a fraction of a millimetre. This caused blurred images to be sent back to Earth	The reason for the flaw was that the company had ignored data telling them the mirror was imperfect, as they thought the instruments measuring the mirror were not sufficiently accurate. In 1993 a correcting package was flown out on the Space Shuttle and fitted by astronauts
TGN1412 drug trial	2006	Parexel drug-testing company and TeGenero, the pharmaceutical company making the drug	Eight healthy male volunteers participated in a clinical trial at Northwick Park Hospital in London. Six suffered severe side-effects, including organ failure. Two, who received placebos, were not affected	The drug had not shown any signs of causing problems, even in animals closely related to humans. There is no evidence as yet that the reaction could have been predicted. Parexel is believed to have followed the proper procedures for drug trials. The men have recovered but may have long-lasting immune-system problems

The variety of erroneous events shows how difficult it can be to get things right, and that being right all the time is impossible. Human error and ignorance of alternative facts both contribute to difficult situations. In the most recent well-publicised example, the clinical drug trial in 2006, stringent conditions and the best possible evidence were followed, but disaster occurred for the volunteers. This indicates that even the best planned experiment, designed on the best possible evidence, can still go inexplicably wrong.

Experimental error

Inevitably, human error plays a part in science too – we can misread a scale, twist a control one stop too far, or turn the gas up just a little bit too high. Any of these can result in a disaster. On occasions, a serendipitous, unexpected, positive or useful result may also occur. These are mistakes – not true experimental errors. Before leaving the topic of error, it is worth addressing the alternative meaning and clearing up this common misconception.

In science, we often talk about 'experimental error'. This means the margin allowed in collecting data, not the role of human error in making mistakes. The extent of error needs to be borne in mind when considering results. Errors can arise from different sources.

- Using mean or average values when doing calculations – a precise value may cause a different result to be produced.
- The limits of accuracy to which an instrument will measure – instruments are calibrated for specific conditions, and/or have scales calibrated to a specific fraction of a gram or metre. We cannot 'read in' more accuracy than the equipment allows. Error can be reduced by using more accurate apparatus.
- Sampling – it is important to make a suitable number of measurements, repeating an experiment a certain number of times, to ensure data are free from bias. What is a 'suitable number' varies. When doing a titration, for example, taking three repeat values is good practice.
- External influences, such as draughts or internal currents, may cause error. For example, when weighing to fractions of a gram, a slight draught may cause fluctuations in the reading. A thermometer may hit a cold or hot spot in a liquid, causing a reading that does not represent the true temperature.
- Simply making the measurement can cause error, for example by introducing a cooling effect or disturbing an animal's metabolism.

◆ Not all measurements have accurate values – the value for the size of a planet, or the distance to a star, will not necessarily be accurate. We cannot make calculations that are any more accurate than the values we use.

◆ *What do we mean by risk and hazard?*

For definitive answers we went to the Health and Safety Executive (HSE) website, www.hse.gov.uk. Its definitions are:

◆ a hazard – any thing that has the potential to cause harm
◆ a risk – the chance that a hazard will cause harm to someone or something.

Examples associated with use of school science equipment and doing experiments are well documented, so are not repeated here.
The HSE also defines:

◆ risk management – the steps taken to reduce the chance, and/or mitigate the consequences, of the hazard causing harm
◆ risk assessment – a careful analysis of what could cause harm.

We take these definitions into account in the following section.

◆ *Sorting risk from hazard: the example of bird flu*

We easily confuse risk and hazard, making bad decisions about what to do as a result. Here we try to clarify the difference using the example of the recent scare about bird flu, avian influenza virus H5N1. The virus can cross the species barrier from birds to humans. Humans infected with H5N1 have died. H5N1 has caused the largest number of deaths of any avian flu virus. This leads to the conclusion that H5N1 is definitely a hazard, as it clearly has the potential to cause harm.
Next, we need to consider the risk – the **chance** that H5N1 will cause harm. This will vary depending on what we do. Someone who works closely with birds, say farming chickens or keeping pigeons, ducks or geese, will be exposed to a higher risk of infection than someone who works in an office. The **hazard** is the same for both people, but the **risk** is different. The risk of infection increases if both people are based in a country where there have already been human cases of H5N1 infection. Again, the risk is much higher for the person working with birds than

for the office worker. This is because scientists have found that H5N1 transfers more easily from birds to humans than from humans to humans. So the people at highest risk of getting H5N1 infections are those working with birds in areas where the bird population is known to carry the virus.

We can interpret UK media reports about birds that have died from H5N1 infection as if this represented a serious risk to us all. We could, on the basis of one or two birds dying, decide to take extreme measures to reduce the risk, such as killing all wild birds, not feeding wild birds, using disinfectants when we have been outside for a walk, and so on. In fact, the risk to the average person going about their daily life is changed only slightly. As people tend to respond emotionally rather than rationally to such reports, panic can set in where this is not necessary. The tendency is to overestimate risk when we are unfamiliar with the context. Conversely, we tend to underestimate risk associated with familiar contexts (see the activity on page 137).

Scientists can introduce new information that may change the picture: these types of virus are known to be able to change their DNA. This could mean that the infection patterns may also change – in the future, human-to-human infections may become more likely. As the viruses do not normally infect humans, few people have immunity to them. Therefore, if the virus DNA did change to promote human-to-human infection, a pandemic is likely. In that case, the risk to us all is enhanced, and more extreme risk management strategies are justified.

This brief analysis shows how risk can change for the same hazard. On one hand, the vast majority of people living in the UK today are at low risk of bird flu infection. On the other hand, this could change – if the virus changes, the hazard increases its potential to cause harm, in turn increasing the risk of infection.

The task of organisations such as the World Health Organization (www.who.int) is to undertake risk assessment on our behalf and to ensure we have correct information to manage risk for ourselves. As far as H5N1 goes, the WHO website is full of advice about outbreaks, offering general guidelines, maps and details of human cases.

Overall, there has to be a balance struck between the cost of reducing the risk and the potential effectiveness of any measures taken. Risk can never be reduced entirely to zero, whatever measures are taken. Good risk management can reduce risks to acceptable levels.

7.4 Teaching about risk, hazard and error

Students need to have a good understanding of how to analyse risk, and the difference between a hazard and a risk. An element of risk is associated with everything we do, including walking up and down stairs, driving a car, cooking and playing sport. Workplaces and schools are hazardous environments. Most of us do not have accidents most of the time, but we are nonetheless still at risk – even if this is often very small.

We think, however, that care is needed. By 'good' understanding, we mean knowing when a risk is genuinely large enough to worry about, and how to distinguish these occasions from scary media stories that overinflate risks. Good science teaching can help redress the balance. Our advice, adapted from the HSE, is to deliver consistent, explicit messages about risk awareness. Discuss risk scenarios with students as they arise, taking the opportunity to address issues as they are presented in the media. More practically, help students to analyse risks associated with everyday activities, such as cycling to school rather than travelling by car. One reason for not cycling is that people perceive a higher risk of accidents. Go through the potential hazards and benefits associated with cycling and travelling by car, together with an assessment of risk. Risk can be managed and minimised – wearing a cycle helmet and reflective clothing, and having lights and a bell, as well as knowing how to ride safely, can all contribute. The first task (page 137) lists a number of different activities that can be used in discussions like this.

In science lessons, we have to take steps to reduce the risk associated with doing practical experiments. Some teachers have believed it necessary, sometimes acting under locally determined orders, to take this to extremes, reducing the amount and nature of practical work to an absolute, simplistic minimum. However, fewer accidents take place in science laboratories than elsewhere in schools. One could argue that this is because science teachers are cautious, but it is also because the risks of accident are much less than we think. We often hear that specific experiments are 'banned' when in fact they are not – the resources section (page 150) lists information that can help promote experiments without unduly increasing risks to students. We would encourage teachers not to use perceived risk as an excuse to prevent students from doing science (and finding out how it works) for themselves. Instead, find out what the true situation is, if necessary challenging a so-called ban and carrying out a proper risk assessment.

Enabling students to handle risk will give them confidence in their ability to make decisions that can influence their daily lives positively. They will be aware of their own and others' abilities to deal with different situations. Understanding risk means that students will know when to seek advice about minimising risk, and where to get it. They will also be able to work responsibly and collaboratively, bearing in mind rules and regulations that support risk assessments. These skills may well be transferable, aiding students as they adjust to workplaces and the general events that life brings.

7.5 Summary

In this chapter, we acknowledge that scientists are prone to error. They may unintentionally promote a discovery that is a hazard without fully analysing the risks involved. These events can cause loss of life, loss of money, problems for the environment, or difficult situations of various kinds. Error is part of how science works.

We show the difference between risk and hazard, and offer opportunities to address these with students using topical contexts.

We have discussed briefly the need to introduce students to risk. We encourage teachers to work positively to help students make accurate assessments of risk. This includes allowing them to do hands-on practical work and participating in other experiments. Teachers need to analyse risk associated with practical work thoroughly, and to be both stimulating and responsible about this aspect of their job.

References and resources

Melamed, A. (2005) *AS Science for Public Understanding*. London: Nuffield Foundation.

General risk-related websites
The Health and Safety Executive: www.hse.gov.uk
HSE's education resources about risk:
www.hse.gov.uk/education/resources.htm

The Royal Society for the Prevention of Accidents (RoSPA) website has a good range of general information to use as background in lessons about risks and hazards: www.rospa.com

The CLEAPPS website has good information about safety in the Science classroom: http://www.cleapps.org.uk/prifr.htm

The thalidomide tragedy

Frances Kelsey's role in preventing approval of thalidomide: www.fda.gov/fdac/features/2001/201_kelsey.html

For a sensitive description of the tragedy, the chemistry, and photographs of children with thalidomide-related defects: www.chm.bris.ac.uk/motm/thalidomide/start.html

The MMR vaccine

An NHS website is devoted to the MMR vaccine, giving a good range of information including references to all the articles that gave rise to the scare, background to the diseases, supporting studies and facts about the vaccine itself: www.mmrthefacts.nhs.uk

Epidemics of measles have been reported in Ireland in 2000: www.irishhealth.com/?level=4&id=380

and in Germany in 2006: www.dw-world.de/dw/article/0,2144,2025964,00.html

The first measles death in the UK for 14 years was reported in 2006: http://news.bbc.co.uk/1/hi/england/4871728.stm

Avian influenza (bird flu)

The Department for Environment, Food and Rural Affairs (Defra) website has a section on avian influenza, where information about the situation regarding bans for movement and trading of birds is updated regularly. There is also a helpline to report findings of dead birds, and information about the effects of the virus on the countryside. This can currently (at the time of writing) be accessed from the Quick links list: www.defra.gov.uk

World Health Organization: www.who.int

WHO's pages relating to avian influenza provide comprehensive information on every aspect of bird flu from an international perspective, including maps, reports and alert-and-response operations: www.who.int/csr/disease/avian_influenza

Index

INDEX